Faith:

EXPERIENCING
The UNIMAGINABLE

Faith:

EXPERIENCING
The UNIMAGINABLE

A 90 DAY DEVOTIONAL ON DEEPENING YOUR FAITH

LORRAINE HILL

TATE PUBLISHING
AND ENTERPRISES, LLC

Scripture quotations marked (NASB) are taken from the *New American Standard Bible®*, Copyright © 1960, 1962, 1963, 1968, 1971, 1972, 1973, 1975, 1977, 1995 by The Lockman Foundation. Used by permission.

Scripture quotations marked (NIV) are taken from the *Holy Bible, New International Version®, NIV®*. Copyright © 1973, 1978, 1984 by Biblica, Inc.™ Used by permission of Zondervan. All rights reserved worldwide. www.zondervan.com

This book is designed to provide accurate and authoritative information with regard to the subject matter covered. This information is given with the understanding that neither the author nor Tate Publishing, LLC is engaged in rendering legal, professional advice. Since the details of your situation are fact dependent, you should additionally seek the services of a competent professional.

The opinions expressed by the author are not necessarily those of Tate Publishing, LLC.

Published by Tate Publishing & Enterprises, LLC
127 E. Trade Center Terrace | Mustang, Oklahoma 73064 USA
1.888.361.9473 | www.tatepublishing.com

Tate Publishing is committed to excellence in the publishing industry. The company reflects the philosophy established by the founders, based on Psalm 68:11,
"The Lord gave the word and great was the company of those who published it."

Book design copyright © 2015 by Tate Publishing, LLC. All rights reserved.
Cover design by Samson Lim
Interior design by Shieldon Alcasid

Published in the United States of America

ISBN: 978-1-68207-123-6
Religion / Christian Life / Devotional
15.09.01

Acknowledgements

Shawn Hill, my beloved husband—my greatest gratitude for the endless support and encouragement you have shown me over the years. Words cannot express how thankful I am for you. You are my treasure.

Noah, Joshua, and Hannah, my sweet children—I love you dearly and am so thankful to be your mother. Thank you for supporting and encouraging me to do the Lord's work. You are so precious to me.

Tricia Owen, Peggy Pickens, Lindy Schuch, Corina Scobercea, Lanette Sikes, Paula Weatherly, my amazing leadership team—I am blessed beyond measure to have such a godly leadership team and to share this ministry with you. You have such a passion and love for our Lord. Thank you for encouraging, challenging, and inspiring me. Thank you especially for painstakingly reviewing, researching, and evaluating this devotional with me. You are a wonderful blessing to me.

Barbara Harlan, Brandi Horton, Melanie Johnston, Penny Kemp, Kristy Wardlow, my sweet friends—your dedication to our Lord is humbling and inspiring. I have been uplifted and strengthened by your friendships countless times. My heartfelt thanks for reviewing this devotional with me.

Contents

Day 1
Our Journey of Faith

And without faith it is impossible to please him, for he who comes to God must believe that he is and that he is a rewarder of those who seek him.

—Hebrews 11:6

Our Christian walk is an exciting journey of faith, the adventure of a lifetime. We will experience more with God than we could ever imagine. Yet, there are also challenging parts to the journey, and we must continually trust the Lord and exhibit faith. So what is faith? The Greek word for faith, *pistis*, means "a firm persuasion, a conviction based on hearing."[1] Faith is more than just intellectual assent or knowledge. It involves obedience. We believe and therefore act upon that belief.

In our lives, we have to choose to walk by faith. It is a choice that we make daily. Many distractions will appear to prevent us from continuing our walk of faith, but we must persevere. Why is faith so necessary to the Christian walk? Hebrews 11:6 tells us that "without faith it is impossible to please him [God]." It delights God's heart when we act in faith. As a parent, I have to confess that I love those moments when my child acts in faith and does what I tell him to do. A few months ago, I told my child to sweep the downstairs of our home, and he did it. There were no arguments, no whining, and no complaining. I cannot tell you the sheer pleasure I felt. In similar ways, our faith pleases God and delights his heart. Can you imagine the sheer joy of pleasing God the next time he calls you to walk by faith?

Faith allows the impossible to become possible, the unattainable to become achievable. It is in our moments of faith that we witness the power of God in our lives and see his miracles. It is in these moments, though difficult and trying, where the glory of God is manifested to the world. So let us step out on faith and ask God for the impossible.

Day 2
Resting in God's Unfailing Love

How priceless is your unfailing love, O God! People take refuge in the shadow of your wings.

—Psalm 36:7 (NIV)

As we walk by faith, we must be careful to not equate our circumstances with God's love. When our circumstances go well, we tend to feel like God loves us; but when circumstances are difficult, we feel God is distant or unloving. The truth, however, is that God's love is constant and enduring. "How priceless is your unfailing love, O God! People take refuge in the shadow of your wings" (Ps. 36:7).

God reminded me of his unfailing love several months ago. One day, I decided to make my children breakfast before school. Now, I have to confess this is not my normal practice; my kids are older and usually make their own breakfast, and I give them a hug as they leave. But this morning was going to be different. So there I was in the kitchen making my kids sprinkle pancakes. As the kids came down for breakfast, they were all surprised; but they ate their breakfast and got ready for school. As they were leaving, my husband looked at me and said, "So now, why did you make them breakfast?" Clearly, he was so shocked by my making breakfast that he thought maybe he had missed their birthday or something. Before I had time to answer, my daughter jumped up and down and said, "Because she loves us!" I smiled at her and gave her the biggest hug, but then I said, "you know I love you even when I don't make you sprinkle pancakes, right?" She said yes, and everyone left. I thought about her reaction all morning and how it related to God. He loves us the same on the day we receive the sprinkle pancakes (the house we want, the promotion, the car, the spouse) as the days when we just get the hug. God's love is consistent in our lives; we just sometimes experience it differently. We must stop walking by how we feel and start walking by what we know. Even though we may *feel* God does not love us, we *know* that he does because Jesus died for us. God's love for us was beautifully settled at the cross!

Day 3
Keeping Our Eyes Fixed on Jesus

Fixing our eyes on Jesus, the author and perfecter of faith.

—Hebrews 12:2a

One summer vacation, my family went to Zion National Park, which is a wonderful hiking park. The first day, my kids and I hiked many of the easy trails and loved it. The second day, however, we chose a more challenging trail. As we started, the trail became perilous with huge rocks in our path, so I told my children to keep focused on the goal. After we climbed to the top, we rested and enjoyed the beautiful view. It was absolutely breathtaking, but I also realized how important it was to keep the right focus. A wrong focus could have easily resulted in hurt or injury.

Our walk of faith will have many challenges, so we must keep our eyes fixed on Jesus or the circumstances of this life will overcome us. In the Greek, the phrase "fixing our eyes" means to look steadfastly and intently toward a *distant* object. We are not to focus intently on our problems or obstacles but rather to focus intently on our Lord. If we are honest, some of the problems in this life are absolutely overwhelming, and constantly focusing on the problems becomes a big black hole that does nothing but drain us emotionally and spiritually. Instead, we need to keep focused on our Lord and rest in him. He is more than able to help us. There is no problem so great that he cannot solve it.

When we truly focus on the Lord, everything else will pale in comparison. In Matthew 17:1–3, Jesus took three of his disciples—Peter, James, and John—to the top of a mountain and was transfigured before them so that they could see his glory. As they gazed at him, I doubt they wondered about the minor problems and difficulties of their lives. Instead, they probably stood mesmerized by the beauty and magnificence of their Lord. That is what we need in our lives—that kind of focus; because if you are like me, it is so easy to become ensnared by this world, its hardships, and its entertainment. When life begins to engulf us and completely overwhelm us, let's make sure we keep our eyes focused on our Lord. Let's picture our Lord lifted up in all his glory and majesty.

Day 4
Choosing to Believe God

And behold, you shall be silent and unable to speak until the day when these things take place, because you did not believe my words, which will be fulfilled in their proper time.

—Luke 1:20

Believing God is a choice. We choose whether we will believe God or whether we will believe the lies of the enemy. Luke

1 reveals the sad story of a man who chose not to believe God and the price he paid for his unbelief. Zechariah, a priest, and Elizabeth, his wife, were a godly couple who loved God, but they also had a terrible heartbreak for Elizabeth was barren and well past the childbearing years. As a couple devoted to the Lord, they cried out to God for a child. Years later, while serving in the Temple, the angel Gabriel appeared to Zechariah and said that God had heard his prayer and granted his wish for a child. How exciting! After years of prayer, Elizabeth would finally conceive.

Unfortunately, Zechariah expressed doubt at Gabriel's declaration, so he was struck dumb for the duration of Elizabeth's pregnancy because he failed to believe God. How sad that as Zechariah left the Temple, he could not verbally share with Elizabeth one of the most exciting moments of their lives. Can you imagine not speaking for an entire pregnancy? I cannot imagine going a whole day without speaking, okay, a whole hour. But an entire nine months? And can you imagine having to explain to others why you cannot speak and that it is because you chose not to believe God? What a daily reminder to Zechariah and to us of the price of unbelief. Unbelief paralyzes us, and we lose innumerable blessings when we choose not to believe God and his promises. Unbelief always steals God's best for us because we settle for an okay or even a good choice but miss the excellent option. It also forces us backward in our Christian walk rather than moving us forward to claim God's great promises.

A great deal of our Christian walk rests here: Do we truly believe God? Do we trust in his promises? Do we take him at his Word? God has such amazing things planned for us, things beyond our wildest imagination; but if we do not exercise faith, we will miss them. Only in faith will we see the impossible and witness the miraculous.

Day 5
Overcoming Unbelief

I do believe; help my unbelief!

—*Mark 9:24b*

We must guard against unbelief because it oftentimes comes prettily packaged through human logic and reason. Yesterday, we talked about Zechariah and his unbelief. When Gabriel told him that Elizabeth would conceive, it seemed reasonable to Zechariah that she would not; after all, she was past the childbearing age. Zechariah looked at his situation, his weaknesses, and his problems. Unfortunately, he forgot to look at his God. But God was greater than his situation; he always is. And what he has promised, he will fulfill (Isa. 46:11). Unbelief always sees the obstacles and the problems; faith sees the opportunities and the powers of God.

Unbelief is serious because it insults the very nature of God. It casts doubt on his character and maligns his trustworthiness. Charles Spurgeon aptly said, "Every other crime touches God's territory; but unbelief aims a blow at his divinity, impeaches his veracity, denies his goodness, blasphemes his attributes, maligns his character; therefore, God, of all things, hates first and chiefly, unbelief, wherever it is."[1] In essence, unbelief calls God a liar because in unbelief, we say, "We do not believe that you can do what you have said." That sounds terrible, doesn't it? I would never intentionally call God a liar, but that is what unbelief does. Think about how much it hurts when someone calls you a liar or misjudges your character. This is what our unbelief does to God.

Unbelief is often so one-sided. We allow our limited understanding over a situation or person to cloud our relationship with God. Because God chooses to act in a way that differs from our view of him, we become upset and forget his past faithfulness. A friend of mine says that whenever she does not understand something or feels that Satan is making God appear in a negative manner, she asks God to give her wisdom and insight so that she can have the right perspective. Let's decide today that we will *choose* to believe God, no matter the difficulties and the circumstances.

Day 6
Leaving a Legacy

Only conduct yourselves in a manner worthy of the gospel of Christ.

—*Philippians 1:27a*

We have before us one of the greatest opportunities ever: to pass down a spiritual legacy to those who come after us. A legacy is "something transmitted by or received from an ancestor or predecessor or from the past."[1] What type of spiritual legacy will we leave for our children and our children's children? Will they see lives of faith or lives of unbelief? Will they see lives of victory or defeat? Will they glimpse the greatness of God through us?

In Philippians 1:27, Paul urged us to conduct ourselves in a manner worthy of the gospel because he knew the gospel's power to transform lives. The Greek word for conduct involves acting in accordance with the laws of a country. Because we are citizens of heaven and not of the earth, we should conduct ourselves in a manner consistent with the laws of heaven. When we do, we provide a powerful, consistent testimony to those around us—friends, family members, church members, coworkers, and our community. Nothing can compare to the power of a consistent Christian testimony, and no amount of pretty words can compensate for the lack of one. We must start living up to our name as Christians and as Christ believers and followers. The following story provides a vivid illustration:

> Alexander the Great, one of the greatest military generals who ever lived, conquered almost the entire known world with his vast army. One night during a campaign, he could not sleep and left his tent to walk around the campgrounds. As he was walking he came across a soldier asleep on guard duty—a serious offense. The soldier began to wake up as Alexander the Great approached him.
>
> Recognizing who was standing in front of him, the young man feared for his life. "Do you know what the penalty is for falling asleep on guard duty?" Alexander the Great asked the soldier.
>
> "Yes, sir," the soldier responded in a quivering voice.
>
> "Soldier, what's your name?" demanded Alexander the Great.
>
> "Alexander, sir."
>
> Alexander the Great then looked the young soldier straight in the eye. "Soldier," he said with intensity, "either change your name or change your conduct."

We must start walking by faith and living up to our great calling. Then we leave a godly legacy for our children and our children's children as well as impact those around us.

Day 7
Embracing God's Truth

Listen to advice and accept instruction.

—Proverbs 19:20a (NIV)

One of the greatest qualities that Christians can possess is a teachable spirit—a willingness to embrace truth, even the truths that we do not like. First, we must be willing to hear God's truth, no matter how difficult or challenging the truth may be. Each of us has our own preconceived ideas and opinions fostered from our backgrounds, interactions with others, and life experiences. These ideas and opinions, however, do not always agree with the Bible, so we must allow the Lord to reveal his truth to us without becoming defensive and antagonistic. We cannot cling to the comfortable if the comfortable is wrong. The truths we like least are often those that we need most. And remember, as God reveals truth to us, his intention is not to hurt or discourage us but rather to edify and encourage our maturity. He knows that truth always brings freedom and lies always enslave. Refusing to accept God's truth will leave us in bondage.

Proverbs 19:20 reminds us that we must not only hear God's truth but also *accept* it. We must allow truth to penetrate our hearts and change our behavior. Sometimes, we are willing to receive truth but on our terms. God, however, gets to determine the means and the manner of our instruction. For instance, we may accept criticism from a friend because we know that our friend loves us and seeks our best interest. But what happens when God chooses to use someone we dislike? We must be willing to learn truth no matter the source of instruction.

Because God's truths are not always palatable, we sometimes embrace the ones we like and harden our hearts to the other ones. Most of us do not intentionally seek falsehood; rather, we seek the kind of "truth" that allows us to remain within our comfort zones. But truth is truth, and we must not artificially separate it. We cannot embrace the truths we like and disregard the ones we do not. A. W. Tozer aptly remarked, "Truth is a glorious but hard mistress. She never consults, bargains or compromises."[1] God's truths are not always easy or palatable, but they are always true and bring great freedom.

Day 8
Using Eternal Eyes, Not Earthly Eyes

As for you, you meant evil against me, but God meant it for good in order to bring about this present result, to preserve many people alive.

—*Genesis 50:20*

In our walk of faith, perspective is crucial because how we perceive situations and people impacts our actions.

Too many times we view situations through "earthly eyes" and not "eternal eyes." What do I mean by earthly eyes? Earthly eyes are focused on our comfort and convenience. They view life through a short-term perspective, the here and now. Eternal eyes, on the other hand, view situations through God's perspective. They focus on eternity and the character that God is building in us. They see situations as opportunities to reveal God's glory to this world. For example, if our neighbor calls us because she has a flat tire and needs our help, is that an inconvenience because it messes up our busy day or is it an opportunity to demonstrate the love of Christ to someone?

In Scripture, I love the story of Joseph because it is a beautiful display of a man who used eternal eyes. Joseph endured great trials and hardships because his brothers sold him into slavery at the tender age of seventeen. Then he ended up in prison because he chose to act righteously and honor God. In the end, God exalted him and placed him in a position where he could either hurt or help his brothers. Rather than succumbing to anger and bitterness, he made the righteous choice and forgave his brothers. Can you imagine forgiving someone, your own flesh and blood, for selling you into slavery, for stealing thirteen precious years of your life? As this occurred, Joseph said the most remarkable thing: "As for you, you meant evil against me, but God meant it for good in order to bring about this present result, to preserve many people alive" (Gen. 50:20).

Joseph had eternal eyes and saw that God was working in him and through him for God's glory. He did not focus on his current situation, the hardships, and the betrayal he experienced, but he trusted that God would work things out for his good. Eternal eyes see the invisible God and patiently cling to his promises. If we truly want to walk by faith, we will have to stop using earthly eyes. God is working in us and through us in ways we cannot even begin to imagine.

Day 9
The Crucible of Time

Wait for the Lord; be strong and let your heart take courage; yes, wait for the Lord.

—Psalm 27:14

Waiting on God is so hard, isn't it? In our minds, we think that we are missing beautiful opportunities, not realizing that the Lord is working in us, through us, and around us. He is changing and molding us. Some of our most profitable times of learning occur during our valleys of waiting. And yet, if we do not understand God's purpose in waiting, we will end up frustrated, discouraged, and feeling abandoned. We will not understand God's greater plan for our life—that our character is more important than our comfort.

Genesis 15–16 reveals a season of waiting that Abraham and Sarah endured. Like any married couple, Abraham and Sarah wanted children, and the Lord assured Abraham that he would have an heir. As the years passed, however, Sarah remained barren. Her patience wore thin, so she suggested that Abraham sleep with Hagar, her maidservant. Satan will often tempt us to short-circuit God's will, dangling another means before us and causing us to stray from our true path. As time progresses, we rely on our wisdom and abilities instead of trusting in the Lord and waiting on his deliverance. Like Sarah, we may even scheme and manipulate to achieve our goal.

Whether we realize it or not, impatience reveals a lack of faith in God. It implies that either God is a liar or incapable of providing for our needs. God had told Abraham and Sarah that he would provide an heir; they only needed to wait patiently on his timing. Impatience often causes us to act hastily, blinding us to the perils of the quick fix. As a result, we can force ourselves into difficult situations and experience unnecessary heartache and pain. So rather than experiencing God's best in a situation, we settle for the world's worst. It is *never* a good thing to move ahead of God, *never*. As we move ahead of God, we are forcing ourselves to settle for an earthly counterfeit instead of experiencing a divine blessing. We must stop listening to those deceitful whispers that beckon us to act. Good things come to those who wait, not to those who impatiently act before God's perfect timing.

Day 10
Expecting the Unexpected

He came to his own, and those who were his own did not receive him.

—*John 1:11*

The King of glory had come. The long-awaited Messiah of Israel had appeared. The promised of ages had finally arrived. But an interesting thing happened when Jesus came to the Jews: most of the Jews did not receive him (John 1:11).

From the earliest of times, the Jewish people had anticipated the coming of a Messiah, a conquering ruler who would establish his kingdom. Parents told their children about the Messiah, passing the story from generation to generation. The rabbis spent their lives studying the Law and anticipating the Messiah. The people even cried out to God to be delivered from their oppressors. For hundreds of years, the Jews steadfastly believed in their Messiah.

Then the Messiah, the true hope of Israel, finally came to her people; but most of her people did not accept him. Why? Because he did not come in a way they expected. Jesus was a Messiah like no other. He confounded the Jewish expectations because he did not come as a conquering king but rather as a lowly servant; and so, many of the Jewish people missed their own Messiah. Though we may struggle to understand how so many Jews could miss their own

Messiah, perhaps instead we need to ask ourselves if we ever miss the workings of God because we expect him to act in a certain way. Do we limit God to our own traditions, cultural backgrounds, and societal norms, and then get upset when he does not respond the way we think? For instance, we may pray for revival and for a great work of God in his people. Then suffering and persecution comes, and we may think that God has not answered us. Church history, however, reveals that most revivals have not come during times of ease and comfort but rather during times of hardship and difficulty. We must be careful to not limit God to our expectations or we can miss his magnificent acts and works. We have to leave room for God to surprise us.

Day 11
Taking Refuge in God's Goodness

O taste and see that the Lord is good; how blessed is the man who takes refuge in him!

—Psalm 34:8

Do you believe that God is good at all times and in all circumstances? Most of us would say that God is good when we receive a job promotion, buy our dream house, or obtain a new car. But is God also good when we receive a job demotion? When circumstances do not happen as we envision, is God still good?

It is vital that we settle the issue of God's goodness in our lives or Satan will use it mercilessly to weaken our faith. Every time we do not receive something for which we have prayed, Satan will whisper against God's goodness, that God is somehow withholding the best from us. Satan will accuse God's motives and malign his character. He will try to sow doubt and uncertainty in us. If we believe that God is holding out on us, then we will end up walking by the flesh and perhaps even taking what we want for ourselves. We will end up defeated and our faith weakened.

On the other hand, if we take refuge in God's goodness, then we know that if God does not give us something, we are not meant to have it. It would hinder us in our walk of faith instead of helping us. Romans 8:31–32 reminds us that God is for us, not a few times, not sometimes, but always, seeking our eternal best. "No good thing does he withhold from those who walk uprightly" (Ps. 84:11b). God does not stand in heaven pitted against us, intentionally seeking to harm us. He is lovingly walking with us and enabling us to stand strong. God gave us his own precious Son to redeem us. What more could he give us to show how much he loves us? If God gave us his best, his beloved Son, then how would he not give us what we truly need now? If God does not give us something, it is not because he does not love us or has forgotten us but rather because it is not in our eternal best interest. Let us take refuge in God's goodness so that we can experience victory in our faith.

Day 12
Cultivating Contentment

Not that I speak from want, for I have learned to be content in whatever circumstances I am.

—Philippians 4:11

Several years ago, I did an activity with our children about discontentment. After dinner, I called my three kids into the kitchen and offered them ice cream. I gave one gigantic scoop of ice cream to each of the first two children. They were incredibly thankful, saying that I was the best mom! Then it happened. I handed the third child a bowl with two gigantic scoops of ice cream. All of sudden, I went from being the best mom to being the meanest mom. Comparison had reared its ugly head. My children were perfectly content with what they received until they compared to what their sibling received. Does that sound familiar? How many times are we content with God's provision until we compare to our neighbor's provision? Then our provision no longer seems quite as satisfying. Some of our joy dissipates as we realize God may have provided a "greater" blessing to someone else. We fail to realize that God's blessing to us is the perfect blessing we need.

Discontentment reveals a lack of faith because we do not trust God's plan for our lives. From all of eternity, God has known where to place us and the circumstances of our lives. He has specifically chosen to give us certain things and not other things. Discontentment is an insult to his great knowledge and wisdom.

We must trust God's wisdom and rest contently in his love for us. There will always be someone who is prettier than us, who possesses more than us, or who seems to have a greater advantage than us. In Philippians 4:11, Paul said he *learned* contentment. Contentment was not something that Paul acquired instantly upon salvation but rather something he learned. Through life's experiences, God taught him how to remain content whether he had little or much, whether exalted or abased. As we reflect more on God's generous provision to us, we will be more content. When we compare with others, we frequently overlook many of the Lord's blessings to us. Rather than focusing on what we perceive we lack, we must concentrate instead on the many blessings the Lord has already bestowed on us. We must embrace God's wonderful plan for us, finding joy wherever the Lord has placed us.

Day 13
Trusting God with the Unknown

Commit your way to the Lord, trust also in him, and he will do it.

—*Psalm 37:5*

William Shedd, an American theologian, once said, "A ship is safe in a harbor, but that's not what ships are for." In our walk of faith, we have to be willing to trust God with the unknown. God did not create us to simply stay safe and watch life pass us by. He created us to trust him completely and to live unreservedly for his glory.

Living by faith means that we may have to give up our easy, comfortable lives. God may call us to leave the business world and work at a church, stay at home and raise our kids, share the gospel with a neighbor, or stand up for God's truth in our workplaces. When God calls us to act by faith, we sometimes have the wrong impression of God. We think that he is trying to take our lives, but the opposite is true—he is helping us to realize what true life is. Too often, we are willing to settle for the little crumbs of this world instead of the feast that God offers us. If we want to experience the unimaginable in our faith, we will have to trust God with the unknown and step out on faith when he calls. When we are willing to lay it on the line, we will see

God do amazing things in our lives. We will see his glory revealed in unimaginable ways.

Corrie ten Boom, a Christian concentration camp survivor, said, "We can trust an unknown future to a known God." You and I may not know what the future holds, but we know our God! The God who is with us daily also goes before us to prepare our paths; we can trust him in the unknown. We are meant to leave our mark on this world, to leave a legacy that points future generations to the beauty of God and not just simply to sit on the sidelines cheering as a fan. So let us be daring in our faith and trust God with the unknown.

Day 14
Living like a Pilgrim

All these died in faith, without receiving the promises, but having seen them and having welcomed them from a distance, and having confessed that they were strangers and exiles on the earth.

—Hebrews 11:13

Scripture repeatedly reminds us that we are pilgrims in this world, aliens and strangers just passing through (Phil. 3:20; 1 Pet. 2:11). Earth is not our eternal home, but too often we live as if it is. We store up possession after possession in our earthly home, giving little or no thought to our eternal home. Sometimes, we even put down roots and dig in, not willing to move where God wants us to move or to do what he commands us because we are afraid to rock the boat. Deep down, if we are honest, we enjoy the comfort and security we have. We forget that this period in our lives is a transitional time, a stepping stone to eternity, the season in which we are being grown and matured.

When I teach, I often use a moving example to illustrate how transitory this world is and how foolish it is for us to invest our time, effort, and passions in something that will soon be gone. Imagine for a moment that I live in Houston but am moving to New York. So I load my moving truck and start on my journey. On the way, I stop in Atlanta and stay in a motel room for the night. While in the motel room, will I repaint the walls, put up pictures, and buy nice accessories? No. Why not? Because it is just a motel room; it is not my home. My new home will be New York. That is all this earth is: the motel room. Please understand that I am not saying that we cannot own pretty things, have a nice house, or decorate our house, but I am saying we need to be careful about how much time and energy we invest in transitory things. They are here today but gone tomorrow. How sad it would be at the end of our lives to realize that we had invested in the temporal instead of the eternal. Let us not be seduced into believing this world is our home. It is merely the stepping stone to heaven and eternity with our magnificent Father.

Day 15
Do Not Overlook the Ordinary

*For we are a fragrance of Christ to God among those
who are being saved and among those who are perishing.*

—*2 Corinthians 2:15*

I truly believe that God intends to do great things in our
lives as we walk by faith. Over the years, however, God has
also convicted me that I am not to overlook the ordinary
parts of life. So many times, I can become so focused on
wanting to see God do "the spectacular" that I can miss
the beauty of "the everyday" things of faith. The ordinary
is not unimportant for God uses the ordinary as well as the
spectacular to accomplish his purposes.

Everyday acts of faith occur when we seek to do God's
will and bring him glory. Here are a few examples of those
ordinary moments because we have far more "ordinary"
moments than "spectacular" moments.

- After a long, tiring day, our child seems to have
  extra energy, constantly asking us questions. Even
  though we are weary and tired, we patiently listen
  to our child and play with him.

- On our way to meet our girlfriends for a fun afternoon, which we have been planning for weeks, we see a lady broken down at the side of the road. We stop to help her but miss our special time with our friends.

- Our neighbor has just been diagnosed with cancer. She is not a Christian and is very distraught with the diagnosis. We decide to make her dinner and to share the love of Christ with her.

- A friend from church, who is a single mother of three, loses her job and is struggling to support her family. We decide to anonymously buy her groceries and leave them on her doorstep, along with a card for encouragement.

- A coworker is mean and demanding, but we choose to act kindly and graciously to her, thereby allowing her to glimpse God in us.

These are all ordinary acts that occur in the everyday, but we make them extraordinary when we choose to follow God's leading and act in faith. Our faith can shine beautifully in both the spectacular moments and in the ordinary moments of this life, so let us be careful to not overlook the ordinary.

Day 16
Victorious in the Warzone

For we are a fragrance of Christ to God among those who are being saved and among those who are perishing.

—Ephesians 6:12

Ephesians 6:12 informs us that we are in a spiritual war and that our struggle is not against flesh and blood but rather the rulers and powers of darkness. The Greek word for struggle, *pale*, means "to shake, vibrate. A wrestling, struggle or hand-to-hand combat."[1] This reveals the seriousness of the battle we face, a hand-to-hand combat. We must never underestimate Satan or his wicked angels. He will use the world, our flesh, our lusts, other people, whatever he can to destroy us.

If we are honest, we rarely picture the invisible spiritual war raging around us, and especially not one in the heavenly realm. We continue our daily activities with little thought to the spiritual war that surrounds us, yet behind the physical realities we see lay spiritual forces that we do not see. For instance, we may have disagreements and fights with other people. What we fail to realize is that Satan often incites people, creating strife and division. It is a sobering thought to think that Satan has incited other people against us and against God's work.

Ephesians 6:11 further informs us that Satan has schemes, and they are not haphazard. They are deliberate, intentional attacks, personally targeting our weaknesses and areas of struggle. What Satan uses for one person, he may not use for another because it does not work. Satan strategically targets our weaknesses and areas of vulnerability. Sometimes he will even use our strengths against us, by trying to create spiritual pride in us. His "best" attacks, however, seem to surface in our isolation and darkness, perhaps because we are in a vulnerable position or low point.

If you are like me, you sometimes get tired of fighting, tired of the difficulties, and tired of the pain. But we must keep fighting. We must keep persevering. We are in a deadly war. The stakes are high. Sometimes I want the victory without the battle. But while evil still exists, there will always be a battle, and we must be willing to fight for what is good and true. Victory is always attainable through God!

Day 17
Knowing God Deeply

But whatever things were gain to me, those things I have counted as loss for the sake of Christ.

—Philippians 3:7

One of the main ways we increase our faith is by deepening our relationship with God. We need to know God—truly know him with not just an intellectual, head knowledge but an intimate, heartfelt knowledge. As we know God more, it allows us to trust him more and to step out on faith when he asks.

So how can we "know" the Lord? As we read the Bible, we acquire a base knowledge of the Lord. Then, as we experience the victories and defeats of life, we begin to experience him personally; this deepens and expands our initial understanding of him. As we speak of "knowing" the Lord, I must issue a caution. We may all know the Lord but to various degrees; the degree indicates the depth of our relationship. For instance, Ruth Graham and I both know Billy Graham, but Ruth had a much more intimate relationship with Billy Graham than I. You see, we can know the Lord and never really know him. We can know who the Lord is and possess a head knowledge of him or we can know the Lord deeply and intimately. We can also know the Lord in the sense that we like him, just as we may like Billy Graham, but never really depend on him in our lives. Ruth loved Billy because she had developed an intimate relationship with him. She depended on him as a husband and daily sought his support. How well do we truly know the Lord? Are we depending on him and seeking his support?

If we want to have a deep relationship with the Lord, we will have to make time for him. If we only talked to our spouse once a week, it would hinder our relationship. The same holds true in our relationship with the Lord. If we only talk with him once a week, we hurt our relationship. Sometimes we want the outcome, a deeply intimate relationship with our Lord, but are not willing to pay the price in terms of commitment, time, and dedication; the result is a halfhearted relationship. We must be willing to make the time for our Lord.

Day 18
Living as Lights

You are the light of the world. A city set on a hill cannot be hidden.

—Matthew 5:14

In Matthew 5:14–16, Jesus provides a beautiful description of Christians: we are lights to this world, revealing the magnificence of God to others. Light illuminates wherever it is. It simply cannot be hidden. We are meant to provide light wherever we are—in our neighborhoods, at work, in grocery stores, at sporting events, in the library, on vacation, wherever we are.

Jesus stressed his point by stating that a person would not light a lamp and place it under a bowl since that would hinder the usefulness of the light. Instead, the light is placed on a stand to provide light for everyone. In a sinful world, we are the light leading others to the Lord. For example, we have friends who were complimented about their children and their parenting skills. Our friends replied that they used the Bible as their main parenting source because it provided the guidance they needed to raise their children. As a result of the discussion, the other couple ended up reading the Bible, which they had never before read. Our friends' light shone brightly and beautifully as they drew others to the Lord and to his Word.

Light, even in the smallest of glimmers, dispels the darkness and brings illumination. Darkness can never put out the light. Are we serving as lights, drawing others to Christ? Are we helping to dispel the darkness? The closer we come to Jesus, the greater our lights shine for we reflect him more.

Light also seems to shine the brightest in the darkest of places. In church, for instance, our light often blends in with the light of other Christians; but in a non-Christian workplace, our light shines brightly. Like a match in a dark cave, a small light can make a big impact on the darkness. As the world sees the hopelessness around them, we serve as its beacons. So be encouraged if you are in a dark place; you can radiate light and impact others for God!

Day 19
Trusting God for the Greater Glory

Jesus said to her, "Did I not say to you that if you believe, you will see the glory of God?"

—*John 11:40*

In John 11, Jesus received word that his close friend Lazarus was dying. One would think that upon hearing this, Jesus would have immediately left for Bethany to see Lazarus; instead, he decided to stay for two more days. Can you imagine the disappointment Mary and Martha, Jesus's close friends, must have felt when Jesus did not arrive on their timetable? Perhaps you have expected God to come on your schedule and have been disappointed when he does not? God is sovereign, and he knows what actions must occur to provide him the greatest glory. He has his own schedule. Though we are frequently rushed, he is not. God always delivers, just not always on our timetable.

Eventually, Jesus arrived in Bethany, but Lazarus had died and been buried in a tomb. Why did Jesus not come earlier? Better yet, why did Jesus not heal from a distance? Why allow his beloved friend Lazarus to die? Because he had a greater glory to reveal—Jesus was going to raise Lazarus from the dead. In Scripture, Jesus only raised three people from the dead: Jairus's daughter, the son of the widow, and Lazarus. Lazarus, however, was the only one who had been in a tomb, probably beginning to decay. Can you imagine the reaction of the people as they witnessed Jesus raise Lazarus to life? Can you imagine how beautifully God's glory was demonstrated? Jesus could have chosen to heal Lazarus before he died, but raising Lazarus from the dead provided a greater glory. In all honesty, we might have been tempted to settle for Jesus merely healing Lazarus, not realizing that he was going to resurrect him. Think of what we would have missed. In this life, when things do not occur on our timetable or when we have to travel a more difficult path, we have to trust that God is working things out for a greater glory.

Day 20
The Knowledge of God

The wonders of one perfect in knowledge.

—*Job 37:16b*

In our walk of faith, we will inevitably face times when we do not understand why God does or does not do certain things. I wish I could tell you that God will always explain himself to us, but he does not; and we have to come to a place where we trust in his wisdom or we will falter in our faith. So let's take a few moments today to understand God's wisdom because this will enable us to trust him when we do not understand our circumstances.

Scripture tells us that God is omniscient, meaning that he knows all things: "His understanding has no limit" (Ps. 147:5b, NIV). God does not possess some knowledge; he possesses all knowledge and has done so for all eternity. Imagine, God knows how many stars lie in the universe, the number of grains of sand on the beaches, and the number of hairs on your head. Truly amazing, isn't it? It would take us years to count the number of grains of sand on the beach, and yet the Lord already knows and has known this information for all eternity.

God knows all things past, present, and future for all people who have ever existed. He also knows events before they happen. Since God already knows all things, events never surprise him as they unfold. Science does not perplex him, and discoveries do not startle him. God has always had perfect knowledge; and unlike us, he has not acquired more knowledge over a period of time. If you are like me, I can barely remember the current events in my life, let alone obscure details from my past; yet God knows all things past, present, and future for all people who have ever existed!

Since God has all knowledge, he can answer us perfectly in prayer. Since he knows our individual strengths and weaknesses, he knows what we need in our lives to bring him glory and to allow us to mature in our walk with him. Thus, he knows if giving us a job promotion would weaken our Christian walk or strengthen it. He knows if marrying that person will help us to draw closer to him or to move further away. We can rest contently in God's wisdom, knowing that he has the "all" perspective and provides those things that are best for us from an eternal perspective and allow us to become more like Christ!

Day 21
The Wisdom of God

Oh, the depth of the riches both of the wisdom and knowledge of God! How unsearchable are his judgments and unfathomable his ways!

—Romans 11:33

Since God has all knowledge of past, present and future, God is able to be wise. Wisdom results from the application of knowledge. We do not have full wisdom because we lack full knowledge. We are limited in the amount of information that we receive and also in the way in which we process such information. We often evaluate situations by our feelings, emotions, or comfort. God's decisions, however, are based on full knowledge, pure righteousness, perfect love, and unbiased justice. This means that God is never wrong when he makes a decision. He is never distracted by his feelings. He never succumbs to sin. God has the big picture, seeing that which we cannot see. As God evaluates our situation, he examines a zillion possibilities and settles on the option that is best suited for us to bring him glory. His choice is always the perfect choice; we just do not always understand it.

We must come to the place in our lives where we trust in the Lord and in his wisdom. We cannot succumb to Satan's deceitful whispers that we know what is best for us. God always desires the best for us from an eternal perspective. What may be acceptable for one person could be devastating to us because we lack spiritual maturity in that area. We all have our weaknesses and blind spots. There are things that we cannot possess because they would hinder our relationship with God. For example, the Lord may entrust wealth to some, knowing it will not affect their hearts. To others, he cannot because he knows that it would subtly divide their affections for him. The Lord loves us so much, and he gives us those things that are best for us *from an eternal perspective.* He would give us every gift possible if we could handle it. In choosing not to give us certain things, it is because they are not the best for us.

God sovereignly rules from the heavens and sees things that we do not see. I wonder, if we stood in the heavens and looked down on our life, would it change our perspective? Would we trust God more? Let's choose today to trust God and his great wisdom in our walk of faith.

Day 22
Stepping Out on Faith

Then Caleb quieted the people before Moses and said,
"We should by all means go up and take possession of it,
for we will surely overcome it."

—*Numbers 13:30*

After four hundred years of oppression and slavery, God delivered Israel from Egypt. Now, Israel stood poised to enter Canaan, the promised land. The land was theirs, but they would have to exercise faith to claim it (Num. 13–14). So Israel sent a scouting expedition that included twelve men who were leaders in their tribes. When the delegation returned, it affirmed the goodness of the land, a land flowing with milk and honey. But then, ten of the men noted some problems: the cities appeared fortified and the people were strong warriors. The negative report swayed the rest of the Israelites, and they rebelled against the Lord, choosing not to claim the promised land. As a result, God disciplined Israel, and no one over twenty years old, other than Caleb and Joshua, were allowed to enter the promised land.

In the midst of the rebels stood two men, Caleb and Joshua, who tried to convince Israel to trust God. They saw the same problems as the other ten men, but they believed God would enable them to take the land. These twelve men saw the exact same thing but had completely different reactions. Sometimes in our walk of faith, we think it would be easier to trust God in different circumstances. But the truth is faith is not about our circumstances but our relationship with God. And it is not that Caleb and Joshua minimized the problems. Faith never minimizes the problems or obstacles of life; it always magnifies God. It understands that God is greater than any situation, person, or problem that we face. It does not disbelieve the problems but rather believes God for deliverance. Faith trusts that what God has started, he will finish. It understands that God's calling always involves his enabling. When we remain focused on God, nothing seems impossible. When we focus on ourselves and this world, however, everything seems insurmountable.

When God calls us to do something, it creates a crossroad for us—we can trust ourselves or we can trust God. We will never regret trusting God. So let's decide today to trust God when he calls us to step out on faith so that we can experience the unimaginable.

Day 23
Trusting God in the Wilderness

Blessed is the man who trusts in the Lord and whose trust is the Lord.

—*Jeremiah 17:7*

The Bible character Caleb has always intrigued me because of his consistent faith in God. Yesterday, we discussed how Caleb chose to believe God despite the other Israelites' unbelief. Unfortunately, Caleb did not receive the fairy-tale ending, at least not in the short-term. He was left to wander in the desert with the other Israelites for forty long years—that is 14,600 days. Can you imagine wandering in the wilderness for 14,600 days not because you sinned but because someone else did?

One of the hardest things in this life is that we sometimes suffer for the choices and sins of others. We live in a fallen, sinful world, and bad things happen to godly people. For instance, a drunk driver hits your car, and your child is hurt. Someone else's bad choice has impacted your family. So what do we do in a wilderness? How do we deal with it? Do we become angry and bitter with God? Do we merely endure it? No, during a wilderness or difficult time, we want to continue to trust God. I am not saying these times are easy, but I am saying we can trust God with them. Sometimes the pain and suffering just cloud our judgment.

We must go back to the basics, to what we know is true. God is faithful; he will never leave us nor forsake us (Heb. 13:5). And he is doing things around us and through us that we cannot even begin to imagine.

Corrie ten Boom, a Christian concentration camp survivor, aptly said, "When a train goes through a tunnel and it gets dark, you don't throw away the ticket and jump off. You sit still and trust the engineer." When we encounter a wilderness or hardship, we do not give up. We sit still and trust our Great Engineer for he is working things out for our eternal good and his glory (Rom. 8:28).

Day 24
Overcoming Worry

Do not worry then, saying, "What will we eat?" or "What will we drink?" or "What will we wear for clothing?"

—Matthew 6:31

Worry and belief are rivals in our heart, warring against each other for supremacy. When worry wins, belief loses. We may not realize it, but worry is actually unbelief because one of the main parts of our walk of faith is to believe God. Worry demonstrates a lack of belief and trust in our Father, and it is a sin. We either do not believe in God's power or do not trust in his ability to solve our problem.

In Matthew 6:25–34, Jesus tells us to not worry about our food, clothing, or the future. He promises to take care of us and to look after all our needs. Please understand that I am not trivializing some of our problems. Our problems are very real, but God's provision is just as real. And what does worrying really accomplish anyway? Does it solve the problem? Does it help the situation? No. And in many instances, it creates unnecessary stress and havoc. Worry is emotionally, physically, and spiritually draining to us. Worse yet, it completely distracts us from the purposes of God. We can trust God to solve our problem. He is a creative God with innovative ways to meet our needs. Our God has indescribable strength, ultimate wisdom, and unimaginable power. He parted the Red Sea in Exodus, made the walls of Jericho fall down in Joshua, rose dry bones from the ground in Ezekiel, healed the sick in Matthew, cast out demons in Luke, and turned water into wine in John.

Life will always have its challenges. It will press us and squeeze us. We live in a fallen world, riddled with sin and its consequences. There will always be things to worry about, but we do not have to succumb to the worry. God's promise to us is tranquility during the difficulties and peace in the storms. He stands as our Protector, Sustainer, and Provider. We cannot squander the blessings of today by worrying about the possible problems of tomorrow.

Day 25
Obeying God's Will Immediately

And he [Jesus] said to them, "Follow me"…Immediately
they left their nets and followed him.

—Matthew 4:19–20

In Matthew 4:18–22, Jesus called Peter, James, John, and Andrew to follow him. At the time, they were busy fishing and trying to provide for themselves. How did the disciples respond? Immediately, they followed him. The disciples left their nets, boats, belongings, family, and friends to follow the Lord. They also left their plans and dreams for the future. They did not overanalyze the situation or prepare detailed listings of the advantages and disadvantages of following the Lord. They simply followed their Lord. What about us? Do we delay in doing the Lord's will? Do we qualify our obedience based on what the Lord is commanding, or do we instantly obey him, regardless of what he commands?

In order to immediately obey the Lord, we must divest ourselves from the belief that the Lord's commands are always convenient. When the Lord called the disciples, they were not idle men lazing around. They were busy fishing and providing a living for themselves. It would have been far more convenient for the Lord to call them after the day had ended when they had taken care of their responsibilities. The Lord's commands are rarely convenient for us. They usually require us to rearrange our plans, sometimes even causing us to forego our personal dreams. I must warn you too that we only view the Lord's commands as inconvenient if we feel we own our time. If we believe instead that the Lord owns our time (as he does), then he has the right to determine the use of our time.

Faith always involves obedience to God's commands—instant obedience. If we delay in fulfilling God's commands, then we are guilty of delayed obedience, and delayed obedience is disobedience. Having children has helped me to understand this principle immensely. For instance, if I asked my child to take out the trash today, I would not be pleased if he did it a week later but then said to me, "I did what you asked." As the Lord commands us, we must obey him. We must have a sense of immediacy in our lives, a sense of urgency to do the Lord's calling. As the Lord calls us to obedience, those calls are defining moments in our faith.

Day 26
Acting with Integrity

A righteous man who walks in his integrity—
How blessed are his sons after him.

—Proverbs 20:7

Integrity is an integral part of our walk of faith. The Hebrew word for integrity, *tom*, means "the state of being complete or undivided." Integrity is completeness or wholeness. It means consistency between our inner self and our outer self. As Christians, there should be consistency between what we say and what we do.

In Scripture, the prophet Samuel was a man who walked in integrity. He was the last judge in a long line of judges, faithfully serving God during a time of terrible wickedness. He was also God's prophet, encouraging the people, explaining God's Word, and rebuking the people when necessary. Even more impressive was Samuel's integrity. It wavered little, if any, in the face of difficulty and wickedness. In 1 Samuel 12:3, Samuel gave his farewell speech to Israel: "Here I am; bear witness against me before the Lord and his anointed. Whose ox have I taken, or whose donkey have I taken, or whom have I defrauded? Whom have I oppressed, or from whose hand have I taken a bribe to blind my eyes with it? I will restore it to you." In his speech, Samuel made a daring statement. He summarized his life and then agreed to right any wrong. Can you imagine having most of the people whom you have ever encountered stand before you and then agreeing to right any wrongs that you have committed against them? The truly amazing part, however, is that not one person stood against Samuel, not one in all the masses. Everyone concurred that Samuel had acted righteously during his life. Samuel chose to remain righteous in unrighteous times, living as a light in a time of darkness. Let me also stress that Samuel did not live a perfect life. He sinned just like you and me, but he acknowledged his sin and sought God's forgiveness. Let's ask God to help us have this depth of integrity in our lives of faith! True integrity does not depend on society, circumstances, or people; it depends on the depth of character within the person. Integrity rises above the wickedness of society, the difficulty of circumstances, and the influence of people. Wicked societies, difficult circumstances, and trying people—these do not wear down our integrity. It is quite the opposite: they allow it to shine beautifully, like a sparkling jewel awaiting the right lighting.

Day 27
God's Silence Is Not His Absence

I cry out to you for help, but you do not answer me;
I stand up, and you turn your attention against me.

—Job 30:20

As we experience trials and hardships in our walk of faith, God sometimes seems eerily silent as we call out to him. We may think that the Lord has not heard us or that he is not listening. Yet, the Lord often makes us wait in order to grow our faith and perseverance. All the while, God is still there, working around us and through us. God's silence is not his absence.

The Old Testament ends with the prophet Malachi, while the New Testament begins with the book of Matthew. In between these two books are about four hundred years. During this period of time, God seemed silent to Israel for he sent her no major prophet. These were not easy times for Israel for she was under foreign rule, first by the Persians, then the Greeks, then the Romans. Israel continued to call out to God, and all the while God appeared quiet. Then, God broke the silence in a remarkable way, and our Messiah, Jesus, was born. During that four-hundred-year time, God was preparing to send Israel her great deliverer. Can you imagine how Israel must have felt during all those years? Can you identify with Israel? Have there been times you have cried out to God and heard nothing?

Oswald Chambers interestingly commented that some of God's silences occur because he trusts us: "When you cannot hear God, you will find that he has trusted you in the most intimate way possible—with absolute silence, not a silence of despair, but one of pleasure, because he saw that you could withstand an even bigger revelation."[1] God's silence is not his absence. During times of silence, God is teaching us humility and growing our faith. In the midst of the reality we see lies a greater reality that we do not see—the work of our loving Father working things out for our eternal good and his glory. Can God trust us with his silence?

Day 28
Standing Strong in Temptation

*And after he had fasted for forty days and forty nights,
he then became hungry.*

—*Matthew 4:2*

If we want to stand strong in our faith, we will have to learn to overcome temptation. In Matthew 4, Jesus had fasted for forty days and forty nights in the wilderness, and then Satan came to tempt him. It is interesting that Satan did not tempt Jesus on day one but rather patiently waited until Jesus was in a weakened physical state. Satan strategically plans his attacks for us, knowing when we are most vulnerable and susceptible to him.

Satan first tempted Jesus by telling him to turn stones into bread. Satan frequently tries to make us question God's care and provision, especially during times of difficulty or hardship. Since Jesus had been fasting for such a long period of time, he was famished. Physical weakness from hunger, illness, or exhaustion usually makes us more vulnerable to Satan's schemes. Since we know such periods weaken our resolve, we must pray in advance for these times. We must also remember that spiritual fulfillment precedes physical satisfaction. The eternal is always more important than the earthly. Jesus did not succumb to Satan's temptation but responded by wielding his sword: the Word of God. The truth of God's Word will always dispel the lies of Satan.

Jesus's resolve did not deter Satan. He merely waited for another opportune moment to strike. Overcoming temptation once does not mean that we will never face it again, so we must remain on guard. After Satan's second temptation, Jesus again quoted the Word of God. Satan tried a third time by showing Jesus all the kingdoms and telling him that if Jesus bowed and worshiped Satan, he could have them. There is always a great temptation to accomplish the Lord's will using worldly means, but we cannot use shortcuts to lessen our difficulties. The Lord's path for Jesus was one of suffering and difficulty, and Jesus could not short-circuit it; neither can we.

After the third temptation, Jesus told Satan to leave him, and Satan left Jesus immediately. No matter what happens in our lives, the Lord has ultimate authority and power. All temptations also only exist for a season; and the Lord, in his sovereignty and mercy, has determined the length of the season. And remember, temptations are not wrong; only succumbing to them is wrong. So let us stand strong during times of temptation.

Day 29
Our Relationship,
Not Our Circumstances

*But I say, walk by the Spirit, and you will not carry out
the desire of the flesh.*

—*Galatians 5:16*

A few months ago, one of my boys hit his brother. When I asked him about it, his response was "He made me do it because he called me a mean name." To which I responded, "No one makes you do anything. You cannot change what happens to you, but you can *choose* your response. Jesus was mocked and beaten, and he did not respond in an ungodly way." This episode made me think. How many times do we try to shift blame when we sin? Are we willing to own our sin and repent, or do we try to subtly shift blame to someone else by saying "He made me do it," "He said something mean," or "He started it"? Sometimes we also try to shift blame to our circumstances: "If my circumstances were different, then I would not sin." The truth, however, is that it is not about our circumstances but about our relationship with God.

Jesus's temptation in the wilderness, which we discussed yesterday, has always fascinated me, and one of the things that stands out to me is how Jesus never succumbed to temptation even though he was in the worst of places: the wilderness. I thought about Jesus in comparison to Adam in the Garden of Eden because both were tempted by Satan. Adam lived in a wondrous garden, enjoying the companionship of his beautiful wife and eating scrumptious food. Jesus was in a desolate wilderness and was hungry. Adam and Jesus were both sinless prior to the temptation, yet the result of the temptation differed vastly for both of them and for us. Adam sinned and brought death on the world; Jesus prevailed and brought life to the world. One might think that with all the comforts that Adam enjoyed, he would have remained faithful to the Lord. Scripture paints another story. It was Jesus, in the desolate wilderness, tired and hungry, who defeated Satan, not Adam enjoying his luxuries in his lush paradise. If we believe that we succumb to temptations because of circumstances, we are wrong. We succumb to temptation and sin because we willfully choose to disobey the Lord. We choose immediate gratification over eternal fulfillment. It is not about our circumstances but about our relationship with God!

Day 30
Allowing the Lord to Lead

The mind of man plans his way, but the Lord directs his steps.

—Proverbs 16:9

In our walk of faith, we can make our plans and have our dreams, but we must be willing to allow the Lord to lead us.

We must give God the freedom to move in our lives and to align our priorities with his. Too often, we make our plans and then ask God to bless them. God created each of us with unique talents and gifts, and he knows how we are to use those gifts and talents best in our lives (Ps. 139).

Sometimes God redirects our steps to ensure that we accomplish his plans and fulfill our destinies. His redirection often comes through interruptions, and we have to be willing to follow these interruptions. Almost every great man and woman of faith was interrupted by God:

- God interrupted Noah's life to build an ark.
- God interrupted Abraham's life to move to a foreign land.
- God interrupted Moses's life to deliver Israel from Egypt.
- God interrupted Nehemiah's life in the palace to rebuild the walls.
- He also did the same with Joseph, Elijah, David, Jeremiah, Mary, and the disciples.

The stories go on and on.

In each of these instances, God interrupted a life, the person followed, and a destiny was fulfilled. Every one of us was created to do works that God determined in advance for us to do (Eph. 2:10). We have a destiny to fulfill, but we will never accomplish it if we do not walk by faith. It will not be easy, comfortable, or convenient, but it will be worth it.

Sometimes we settle for our safe, comfortable lives because we do not realize the greatness that awaits us. Imagine you are hungry for dessert and someone offers you a packaged chocolate chip cookie. We might take it, hoping that it will hit the spot. Now imagine if someone offered you a freshly baked triple chocolate cake. Most of us would take the cake. Sometimes we settle for comfortable lives (the cookie) because we cannot imagine the greatness of what awaits us (the rich cake). In this life, there are good plans, and then there are God plans. We want the God plans and not just to settle for the good plans. So the next time God interrupts our lives, let's be willing to follow.

Day 31
Refusing to Conform to the World

And do not be conformed to this world, but be transformed by the renewing of your mind.

—Romans 12:2a

To live by faith, we will have to stop being conformed to the world in which we live. What does it mean, to "conform?" It means to accommodate our behavior to a certain set of standards. The world in which we live has a very different value system than God. For instance, the world says, "Don't get mad. Get even." "Premarital sex is okay." "Lie and cheat to get what you want." The world wants to conform Christians to its ways, its thinking, and its patterns. If we allow ourselves to be conformed to it, it will subtly begin shifting our values and beliefs.

Sometimes our thinking and values can become subtly conformed to the world's values without us realizing it. The world's standards soon become our standards; its ideals, our ideals. For instance, as we ascend the corporate ladder, we may become enamored with success and material possessions. Slowly over time, we may desire success at the expense of going to church and reading the Bible. Because the world subtly infiltrates our thinking, we must diligently guard against it or we will find ourselves entrapped by it and conforming to it. We should be influencing the world for Christ; the world should not be influencing us.

As I reflect on this verse, you know what strikes me? Why would I want to be conformed to something that will not last? First John 2:17 reminds us that this world and all it encompasses is passing away. Why be conformed to a world that is passing away? Would it not be better to be transformed into something that has lasting value?

The world is continually seeking to push us into its mold. If we are Christians, however, we will never truly fit into this world. Scripture repeatedly describes us as aliens, strangers, and pilgrims. Earth is not our home. We must stop trying so desperately to fit into a world in which we were never meant to fit. Let us refuse to be defined by the society in which we live. Let us refuse to conform to this world and its standards. Instead, let us transform it for God.

Day 32
Embracing True Greatness

Whoever wishes to become great among you shall be your servant.

—*Matthew 20:26b*

Few of us are immune from the provocative allure of greatness. If we are honest, deep in our hearts, we desire fame, to be noticed and acclaimed by others. And yet, Jesus's model of greatness is the opposite of what we might expect. True greatness in Jesus's view is based on servanthood, not self-exaltation. It entails serving others, not being served, and embodies humble, sacrificial service. We will never be victorious in our walk of faith until we understand greatness from Jesus's perspective.

In Matthew 20, Jesus elaborated on his view of greatness. Salome asked Jesus if her sons, James and John, could sit at his left and right hand. Jesus responded by simply saying that it was not his to grant. In his answer, Jesus did not condemn the desire to be great but rather established the parameters for it. The disciples viewed greatness in earthly terms of high position, power, prestige, and fame. Jesus, on the other hand, viewed greatness in terms of servanthood: "Whoever wishes to become great among you shall be your servant" (Matt. 20:26b). Jesus's view of greatness was a model like no other. Rather than pride, he wanted humility. Rather than being served, he desired service. Rather than greatness, he expected lowliness. A. W. Tozer aptly notes, "The essence of his [Jesus's] teaching is that true greatness lies in character, not in ability or position."[1] Greatness is not sitting at the top and allowing others to serve us; it is sitting at the bottom and serving others. Through our service, we should be receding into the background and allowing our Lord to receive prominence and glory.

Jesus created a complete upheaval in the disciples' view of greatness. For the disciples, who have long awaited a ruling Messiah, to now be told to serve rather than to rule was quite startling. Yet Jesus reinforced his view of greatness by saying that even he, God Himself, had not come to be served but rather to serve (Matt. 20:28). Do you find your view of greatness more like the disciples or like Jesus? Do you need to spend a few minutes in prayer asking God to change your view of greatness?

Day 33
Stripped of Supports

Some trust in chariots and some in horses, but we trust in the name of the Lord our God.

—*Psalm 20:7 (NIV)*

In our walk of faith, we are meant to trust in God and God alone. And yet, most of us have crutches in our lives, things that we trust in rather than God. Sometimes, to help us refocus on him, the Lord slowly removes our crutches. And there we lie, stripped of our supports, bare before him, open and vulnerable; but in this vulnerable state, there is great beauty for we are finally learning to trust in only God.

When I think of this process, my mind naturally gravitates to David. He had just defeated Goliath and was placed in King Saul's palace. This was a sweet time for David. But the winds of change blew, and David was soon stripped of his supports.

- *The Elimination of Position.* The first support that was removed was David's position from the palace. Because of King Saul's envy, David had to flee the palace. Position, status, power—all have the potential to intoxicate us. We soon embrace them, becoming accustomed to the advantages that they bring and slowly transferring our trust to them.

- *The Removal of Material Possessions*. With his departure from court, David also lost access to material possessions. Scripture repeatedly warns of the temptation to trust in riches instead of our Lord. They have a tendency to subtly shift our trust from the Lord to them.

- *The Loss of Companionship*. When David fled the palace, he also lost the loving companionship of his wife, Michal, and his friend, Jonathan. During some of David's most difficult times, he would be without the benefit of a loving wife and a great friend. Though others can serve as our confidantes and comforters, they must never take the place of our Lord.

Because of Saul's desire to kill David, David spent years on the run, living in caves and surviving on the basics. During this time, David learned to live each day trusting God. Some of us have become inoculated from trusting *daily* in the Lord by the ease and comfort of our society. Thus, when God removes our crutches, they seem a crushing blow to our lives. During these times, we must remember that God's intention is not to harm us but rather to enable us to see past the temporary nature of this world and to focus on eternity. And these times are actually wonderful moments with God. We experience a greater intimacy with God and a deeper level of faith. With all the crutches removed, the Lord works most profoundly to shape us into the people of God he wants us to be.

Day 34
For Such a Time as This

And who knows whether you have not attained royalty for such a time as this?

—*Esther 4:14b*

By God's providence, an orphan Jewish girl named Esther became the queen of the Persian Empire. It was a privilege of immense proportions. God, however, did not elevate Esther to her position merely so that she could enjoy the benefits of being a queen; he had a far greater purpose than that: God intended to use her to save the Jewish nation.

An evil man named Haman was able to convince King Xerxes, the ruler of the Persian Empire, to sign an edict to kill the Jews. In an effort to save the Jews, Mordecai, Esther's cousin, approached Esther and informed her of what had happened, stating, "Do not imagine that you in the king's palace can escape any more than all the Jews. For if you remain silent at this time, relief and deliverance will arise for the Jews from another place and you and your father's house will perish. And who knows whether you have not attained royalty for such a time as this?" (Esther 4:13–14). Mordecai reminded Esther of two important things. First, deliverance would still come whether Esther chose to help or not for God would protect his people. When we choose not to do God's will, God still accomplishes his purposes, but we lose the blessing.

Second, Mordecai told Esther that her position in the palace did not happen by chance. God had placed her there "for such a time as this." All along, God had divinely orchestrated events in her life to bring her to her position; after all, who could imagine that a Jewish orphan could ever become queen? Like Esther, each of us has a unique place in history. God could have chosen for us to be born at any time, but he chose for you to be here at this time in this generation for a reason. God has divinely orchestrated events in our lives to place us where we are, and we are meant to fulfill our callings. We are called to something greater than ourselves: to do God's will and to make known his glory. We are here for such a time as this. Let us leave our mark on this generation!

Day 35
Having Friends for the Journey

Therefore encourage one another and build up one another, just as you also are doing.

—1 Thessalonians 5:11

Friendship is one of the great blessings in our walk of faith. Friends help us when we fall down, they love us unconditionally, they support us, they uplift us, and they encourage us in our faith. Since friends play such a vital role in our lives, we must exercise discernment in who we allow into our inner circles because our friends have the power to significantly affect our

Christian walk. Our closest friends should be believers; they should be like-minded and possess a similar love and devotion to our Lord. It can be difficult to follow God's will if our non-Christian friends do not see the value in serving God.

True godly friendships must be built on Christ. He must serve as our foundation. Sounds basic, doesn't it? And yet too often, we build our friendships on the things of this world, our hobbies, television shows, decorating for our houses, our clothes, work, and so on. By focusing on earthly and passing things, we can often lose sight of the most important thing: our fellowship in Christ. Rather than remaining as the core part of our friendship, it becomes a secondary component. When we focus on Christ, however, we walk away from our friends feeling spiritually refreshed and renewed by their presence.

True godly friendships also include honesty and openness. We accept others where they are in Christ and help them to mature spiritually. We do not judge their past sins or failures but love them unconditionally. This means being truthful, though at times it may be uncomfortable. As godly friends, we do not sympathize with sin but kindly and lovingly rebuke it. We help our friends as they start to veer off course or become seduced by earthly things. Do we have friends that love us enough to confront us as we sin, who challenge our thinking if it is wrong, and who push us to develop our full potential? That takes a true godly friend. If we are unsure about our friendships or need godly friendships, then we should pray about them. The eternal value of godly friendships simply cannot be overstated. We must have friends who are zealous for the Lord and who spur us on to grow in our faith.

Day 36
God Is with Us

When you pass through the waters, I will be with you; and through the rivers, they will not overflow you. When you walk through the fire, you will not be scorched, nor will the flame burn you.

—Isaiah 43:2

Are you going through a difficult time? Do things seem tough? Are you overwhelmed? Be encouraged—the Lord loves you and will see you through it. His grace, mercy, and peace are there for you, and they are there in abundance! No matter what is happening in your life, the Lord is with you every step of the way. He understands your situation, your pain, your sorrow, and your suffering. He is there for you, and he will sustain you. "Even to your old age I will be the same, and even to your graying years I will bear you! I have done it, and I will carry you; and I will bear you and I will deliver you" (Isa. 46:4).

In Isaiah 43:2, the Lord comforts and encourages us by telling us that he is with us during the difficulties and trials of life. In fact, one of Jesus's beautiful names in Scripture is *Immanuel*, which means "God with us." He is with us through the good times and the bad, the mountaintops and the valley bottoms. Notice, however, that these hardships are expected; thus, the Lord says "when," not "if." Trials are an inevitable part of our Christian walk. James tells us that we should consider it "pure joy" when we face trials because they help to refine our faith and develop our character (James 1:2–4). Unfortunately, there are no shortcuts to spirituality. There are some things that can only be learned in the valleys of adversity. Trials prove the genuineness of our faith, testing what we believe.

Sometimes our trials or hardships cause us to spiral downward. There seems to be no hope, no light at the end of the tunnel. It is at these darkest moments that we need to trust in the Lord the most. Satan would like nothing more than for us to become discouraged and disheartened or to turn away from the Lord during a difficult or trying time. But trials do not have to defeat us; quite the contrary, they are meant to develop us and to make us more like Christ.

Day 37
Dealing with Disappointment

The Lord is near to the brokenhearted and saves those who are crushed in spirit.

—*Psalm 34:18*

Disappointments—our lives sometimes overflow with them. We lost the promotion that we desperately wanted.

The cancer has returned. A long-time friend has divulged our personal information. Our spouse cheated on us. Our child has chosen an ungodly path. Though disappointments may naturally arise, they create a great crossroad for us. We can either continue to trust in the Lord or we can dwell on the disappointments and become embittered and disillusioned by them.

To keep from being discouraged during times of disappointment, we need to pray to our Lord. He can provide us with the wisdom that we need to handle the disappointment and discernment for what to do next. Let's also be honest in our prayers and pour out our hearts to God. The Lord knows how crushing some of our disappointments are; he knows the overwhelming sadness and heartbreak that we feel. Let's allow the God of all Comfort to console us during these times.

Satan seems to wreak havoc with many of us when we are faced with disappointment. And because we are in such a fragile and vulnerable state, we are most susceptible to him. Perhaps one of his greatest techniques is to create doubt in our minds. Has God abandoned me? Why has God allowed this to happen? How can God allow me to experience this disappointment and still love me? Slowly, Satan's whispers become seductive enticements. We should have stopped listening at the first whisper, but we did not. Now we are down the well-worn path of doubt—doubt about God's love for us and doubt about our faith.

To combat Satan's lies, we must arm ourselves with the great truths of God. Our best defense during times like this is the truth of God's Word and the power of God's promises. Though the temptation to wallow in self-pity is great, we must never forget that God is greater than any disappointment that we experience and any sorrow that we feel, and whether we realize it or not, he is working things out for our eternal good.

Day 38
Living without Reservation

Then Jesus said to his disciples, "If anyone wishes to come after me, he must deny himself, and take up his cross and follow me."

—*Matthew 16:24*

Several years ago, I came across the following statement of commitment made by an African pastor in Zimbawe. I encourage you to read it carefully and thoughtfully.

I'm part of the fellowship of the unashamed. The die has been cast. I have stepped over the line. The decision has been made. I'm a disciple of His and I won't look back, let up, slow down, back away, or be still.

My past is redeemed. My present makes sense. My future is secure. I'm done and finished with low living, sight walking, small planning, smooth knees, colorless dreams, tamed visions, mundane talking, cheap living, and dwarfed goals.

I no longer need preeminence, prosperity, position, promotion, plaudits, or popularity. I don't have to be right, or first, or tops, or recognized or praised, or rewarded. I live by faith, lean on His presence, walk by patience, lift by prayer, and labor by Holy Spirit power.

My face is set. My gait is fast. My goal is heaven. My road may be narrow, my way rough, my companions few, but my guide is reliable and my mission is clear.

I will not be bought, compromised, detoured, lured away, turned back, deluded or delayed.

I will not flinch in the face of sacrifice or hesitate in the presence of the adversary. I will not negotiate at the table of the enemy, ponder at the pool of popularity, or meander in the maze of mediocrity.

I won't give up, shut up, or let up until I have stayed up, stored up, prayed up, paid up, and preached up for the cause of Christ.

I am a disciple of Jesus. I must give until I drop, preach until all know, and work until He comes. And when He does come for His own, He'll have no problems recognizing me. My colors will be clear. [1]

The challenge for us is to not merely read these words and applaud the sentiments but rather to ingrain the words in our hearts and live them out fully in our walk of faith.

The African pastor who wrote these beautiful words was eventually martyred for his commitment to Christ. He lived a life of faith and was devoted to God, consumed by his glory. He did not count the cost too high. I pray that we do not either.

Day 39
The Hall of Faith

The world was not worthy of them.

—Hebrews 11:38a (NIV)

Hebrews 11 is commonly referred to as the Hall of Faith because it lists various men and women who walked by faith and so serve to encourage and challenge us in our faith. For instance, Gideon reminds us that God uses the weak so that he is shown strong. Thus, we need never fear when we find ourselves in places of weakness and helplessness; our powerlessness only displays God's powerfulness and our frailty beautifully demonstrates his strength. Joseph challenges us to move beyond places of anger and bitterness with our hurts and to realize that God will bring good out of some of our most hurtful experiences. Rahab encourages us to live by faith, even when it seems that God asks the unusual. She reminds us that God's ways are not our ways nor are his plans our plans. She also shows us that

God can redeem the most sinful of pasts and bring beauty out of them.

One of the most interesting parts, however, comes at the end of Hebrews 11, where it says, "Some faced jeers and flogging, and even chains and imprisonment...They went about in sheepskins and goatskins, destitute, persecuted and mistreated—the world was not worthy of them" (Heb. 11:36–38a, NIV). Did you catch those last few words? They are some of my favorite words: "the world was not worthy of them." As we walk by faith, the world will probably not applaud our efforts or award us prizes. Earthly obedience does not always correspond to earthly rewards. Quite the opposite can happen. We can lose a job for acting with righteousness. We can become excluded from "the girls" because we do not contribute to gossip. We can feel alienation from neighbors because we do not participate in certain activities or conversations. Some people may ridicule us, some may seek to hurt us, and some may even try to persecute us. We will not receive our rewards from this world, and we must stop trying to seek them here. No, the value of our faith will be evidenced in eternity.

What a great encouragement to us that just because the world does not value us does not mean that God does not value us. The world was not worthy of the saints in Hebrews 11, and it is not worthy of us either as followers of Christ.

Day 40
Seeking to Please God

For am I now seeking the favor of men, or of God? Or am I striving to please men? If I were still trying to please men, I would not be a bond-servant of Christ.

—Galatians 1:10

To walk by faith, we have to please God and not man. Easier said than done, right? I will confess that I have wasted far too much of my life seeking to please others at the expense of pleasing God. Several months ago, I was doing my makeup, and my son asked me why I wear makeup. I responded by saying, "Because it hides the wrinkles and makes me look prettier." To which he responded, "So is that a lie then?" Ahhh, children, you have to love their transparency. As I reflected more on what my son asked, I realized that part of the reason I wear makeup is because I am not secure in who I am, and I desire the approval of others. Sounds silly, right? But perhaps you do other things to gain the approval of people?

Embedded within many of us is the desire to please others. We want others to like us. We want them to think nice thoughts about us. In Galatians 1:10a, Paul says, "For am I now seeking the favor of men, or of God? Or am I striving to please men?" Paul reminds us that we need to seek to please God and not men.

Pleasing others at the expense of pleasing God emotionally and spiritually enslaves us in our journey of faith because it inhibits us from doing God's will. In hoping to gain other people's acceptance, we often conform to the peer pressure around us. We think others may laugh at us or mock us, so we refrain from doing or saying certain things. We worry we will lose friendships, so we never allow people to see the real us. We will never fulfill God's plan for our lives if we seek other people's acceptance over God's acceptance. We have an audience of one, the King of kings and Lord of lords, so why do we continually bow before men? Why do we spend so much time and money trying to gain their acceptance? Let us instead rest in God's unconditional love and acceptance of us, and then we forge forward in our walk of faith!

Day 41
Freedom in Our Faith

It was for freedom that Christ set us free.

—Galatians 5:1a

A professor of world religions once said, "Christianity is the hardest religion to live. It has too many rules and regulations; too many demands and requirements." As I reflected on his statement, I realized that this is how much of the world views Christianity—a religion with rules to follow; a burdensome, hard religion. Without Christ, this man is absolutely right; but with Christ, it is a completely different story. Christianity is not harsh, oppressive, or burdensome. It is quite the opposite—freeing, joyous, and exciting. It is not always easy, but it is always freeing. Christianity is not about rules as much as it is about a relationship with God and that relationship brings tremendous freedom!

In Galatians 5:1, Paul reminds us, "It was for freedom that Christ set us free; therefore keep standing firm and do not be subject again to a yoke of slavery." Here Paul specifically referred to the slavery of legalism, but Christ's freedom goes beyond just legalism. He provides freedom in every area of our lives—freedom from sin, freedom from fear, freedom from stress, freedom to become the people we were destined to be. If you remember nothing more from today's devotional, then remember that God's desire in our lives is freedom: complete, glorious, abounding freedom, a freedom that allows us to know God to the greatest degree possible and to experience true life in this sinful world.

Because Christ died, we have been given freedom from our pasts. Our pasts have been wiped clean; they are at the foot of the cross. There is no condemnation for those who are in Christ Jesus (Rom. 8:1). There is no sin so great and no failing so terrible for which we cannot be forgiven. How freeing is that—that we do not have to allow one moment in time, one bad mistake, one terrible choice, to define us? Satan would like nothing better than for us to wallow in our failures and mistakes and to quit, but we cannot allow our pasts to defeat us. Victory has already been given to us through the Lord himself. We do not have to be a prisoner of our past; God has set us free from that. Even more importantly, God sees what we cannot see. He sees our possibilities, our maturity, and our magnificent future.

Day 42
Freedom in Everyday Living

So if the Son makes you free, you will be free indeed.

—*John 8:36*

When God redeemed us, he not only provided freedom from our pasts, as we discussed yesterday, he also provided freedom for everyday living, freedom to live victoriously in Christ. We do not have to wait until eternity to experience the abundant, victorious life. That is God's promise for us today—if we will accept it. We have freedom to live by the Spirit, freedom to do and be who God from all of eternity created us to be, freedom to please and love God with all our heart. Let me clarify, however, that freedom does not mean that we can do whatever we want and sin, because sin and disobedience always brings us back into bondage. So, for example, I cannot get drunk every night. That is not freedom; it is bondage to sin and this world. God did not give us the Holy Spirit so that we would remain in bondage to sin but so that we could overcome sin through the power of the Holy Spirit. God loves us so much that he wants us to experience freedom so we are no longer enslaved to sin and the things of this world. There is freedom about not worrying and stressing about things because God has said he will take care of us. There is freedom from other people's expectations of us, their judgments, and their criticisms because we know that God loves us and accepts us unconditionally. How much time do you think we waste in our lives worried about what others think of us?

I love the story of how a caterpillar changes into a butterfly. Imagine, for weeks a caterpillar crawls on the ground until the day it begins to change. Eventually, it becomes a butterfly and flies with such beauty and freedom. It would be silly for that butterfly to start crawling on the ground like a caterpillar, wouldn't it? And isn't it just as silly that we, as Christians, who have experienced freedom, would then return to a life of bondage? "So if the Son makes you free, you will be free indeed" (John 8:36).

Day 43
Fountains of Life

The mouth of the righteous is a fountain of life.

—Proverbs 10:11a

Proverbs 10:11 reminds us that our mouths should be fountains of life. We should be using our tongues to encourage and strengthen others and to glorify the Lord. For instance, we can use our tongues to witness to unbelievers and to share God's Word with others. We can lift up the Lord in our workplaces. We can discuss God's Word with friends and family. We can encourage others to grow and mature in their faith. We can use our tongues to provide wisdom and instruction to others. "The mouth of the righteous flows with wisdom" (Prov. 10:31a).

We can also use our tongues to encourage one another. In our world, it is easy to become discouraged and downcast. Each of us can probably recall harsh words that have been said to us that have demeaned and discouraged us. We desperately need to encourage each other; a word here and a word there can bring light and laughter to someone who is in the midst of a difficulty or hardship. Our words have the potential to inspire others, to offer comfort and provide hope. There is a world of difference between using words like "stupid," "moron," or "I can't believe you did that, you idiot" and using encouraging words like "Thanks for trying," "Great job," or "I appreciate your hard work." Through our words, we want to bring out the best in others, not the worst.

Even more exciting, we can use our tongues to praise God! Our lives are meant to be full of praise and thanksgiving for God has done so much for us, starting with redeeming us from our sinful lives. Let's take a few moments every day to thank God for his graciousness.

Our tongues should serve as fountains of life. They should nourish, refresh, and encourage others. It is said that we use approximately thirty thousand words a day. How many of those words are we using to glorify the Lord and build up other people? Are we providing much needed refreshment and support? Are we fountains of life?

Day 44
Using the Shield of Faith

In addition to all, taking up the shield of faith with which you will be able to extinguish all the flaming arrows of the evil one.

—Ephesians 6:16

In Ephesians 6:16, Paul revealed a vital part of our spiritual armor as Christians—the shield of faith. Since we are in a spiritual battle, we need spiritual armor. In Roman times, a shield was about four feet long by two and a half feet wide; it was a large oblong shield that protected almost the whole body and blocked the enemies' arrows. It was usually made of wood and covered in leather, which had been coated in water, to deflect fiery darts and flaming missiles. Sometimes as many as two hundred arrows could be launched at a single shield.

Fear, doubt, confusion, unbelief, guilt, shame, temptation, false teachings—these are just a few of the fiery darts that

Satan aims at us. Can you imagine two hundred arrows coming toward us in succession? Scripture describes Satan as the "father of lies" (John 8:44), and he will whisper some of his greatest lies to us if we let him, with fiery arrow after arrow: *God does not love me or he would not have allowed this to happen. God has forgotten about me. God will not forgive me not this time. I am asking for the impossible. This sin will not hurt me this one time.* And the arrows just keep on coming. We must use our shield of faith to deflect Satan's darts or we will succumb to his vicious schemes. Since we are in a spiritual war, the arrows are to be expected, which is why God has provided the shield of faith. It is not enough to know that the shield exists; we must use it.

Interestingly, Roman soldiers often fought in a line, shield to shield. What a wonderful reminder that together we can help each other deflect some of Satan's arrows. Where one Christian is weak, another Christian may be strong, so the strong should help the weak. If you are like me, I have spent far too much of my time not using my shield correctly. I have listened to far too many of Satan's lies and have lived in defeat when victory was around the corner. Isn't it time that we started using our shield of faith and stopped falling for Satan's lies? Isn't it time we started experiencing victory instead of defeat? So let's remember to actively use our shield of faith.

Day 45
Letting Go of Unrighteous Anger

And to those who were selling the doves he said, "Take these things away; stop making my Father's house a place of business."

—*John 2:16*

In John 2, the Passover time had arrived, and Jesus entered the Temple area. Upon seeing the people's wicked and greedy behavior, however, he became angry and overturned the money changers' tables. Then he made a whip out of cords, driving the people and animals from the Temple. As Jesus did this, he did not politely ask the money changers to leave. He was not just a little upset; he was furious. Yet Jesus did not sin in his anger for his anger was a righteous anger in which he was indignant for the dishonor given to the Lord.

So is it permissible to become angry? Is anger a sin? Scripture speaks of two types of anger: *righteous anger* and *unrighteous anger*. Righteous anger occurs when we are zealous for God and for his cause, and it is permissible. Unrighteous anger happens when we feel our rights have been violated. Many times, we automatically assume our anger is warranted and we feel righteous in our anger, but it is often unrighteous. Yet Jesus was not angry for his personal rights and dignity (he was mocked and beaten before Pilate and never justified himself), only for the rights of the Father. It is a slippery slope between righteous and unrighteous anger. What may start out as righteous anger can easily become unrighteous and selfish anger if we dwell on it too long.

Scripture repeatedly warns us to be slow to anger because God knows our great propensity to sin in our anger. He knows how easily we can take a righteous cause and allow it to become self-righteous. To help differentiate between righteous and unrighteous anger, we can ask ourselves some probing questions: What motivates our anger? Are we zealous for God or for ourselves and our rights? We can also honestly ask our Lord. The Holy Spirit will easily affirm our righteous anger by providing peace in our hearts; he will also rebuke any unrighteous anger by providing great conviction.

Day 46
Strengthened by God's Immutability

For I, the Lord, do not change.

—*Malachi 3:6a*

God is immutable, which means he does not change. He will always remain the same. God does not grow or mature nor does he weaken or decay. He does not gain more divinity over time or lose some of his divinity at other times. He is the same yesterday, today, and tomorrow. For all the times we have changed in our lives, God has never changed, not once, not even for one second. There is no variableness or changing in him at all. He is our great constant, our stability, our rock.

God's immutability should comfort and strengthen us in our faith. Because God does not change, he will always love us. We never have to doubt that he will stop loving us, acting mercifully toward us, or being gracious to us. It also means that God is faithful to all his promises. "Not one of the good promises which the Lord had made to the house of Israel failed; all came to pass" (Josh. 21:45). God's most important promise to us involves salvation. He promised a Redeemer and sent his own Son as the atoning sacrifice for our sin. God is also true to his other promises—promises of forgiveness, promises of rest, promises of freedom, promises of meeting our needs, and promises of loving us unconditionally and caring for us. Whether it is the little promises or the big ones, God is faithful to every single one of them.

Because God does not change, we can always rely on him. Too often, we rely on those in the world instead of our Lord; and unfortunately, they can let us down. Friends, family members, coworkers, ministers—they can all make mistakes; they can all cause us pain and heartache. Though not intentionally, they can fail us. God, however, never fails us. We can always depend on him. What peace and comfort we experience from knowing that God is faithful to his promises to us. We can live our lives confidently and expectantly as we trust and rest in God.

Day 47
Valuing God and the Things of God

Thus Esau despised his birthright.

—Genesis 25:34b

In our Christian walk, we will all experience difficulties and hardships. Sometimes life simply overwhelms us, and we want to run for the hills. But if we will learn to value God and the things of God more than the things of the world, we will remain committed to God during those hard times.

Genesis 25 tells the tale of two brothers—Esau and Jacob. Esau was a skillful hunter and fisherman, while Jacob was a quiet and artistic man. One day, Esau arrived home hungry after hunting in the open country. Smelling Jacob's stew, he requested some; but Jacob responded by asking Esau to sell him his birthright. With little thought, Esau agreed and sold it. So for a few tasty morsels of lentil stew, Esau sold his entire inheritance. We can certainly understand that after a long, hard day of being outdoors, Esau would arrive hungry and famished. What is not so easy to understand is why he would willingly forego the blessings of God for some stew. Surely there was other food available, perhaps some leftover bread from breakfast?

Genesis 25:34 informs us that Esau *despised* his birthright; he simply did not value it. Hebrews 12:16 provides additional insight into Esau's character, calling him *immoral* and *godless.* Esau focused on earthly things, not eternal things; but the spiritual should always take precedence over the physical, the eternal over the earthly.

It honestly surprises me that Esau would willingly trade his birthright for a bowl of soup, that he would so despise the Lord. The Lord, however, graciously reminds me of how I can also despise him:

- When I value the pleasure of my sin over the beauty of his holiness, I have despised him.

- When I seek my fulfillment over performing his will, I have despised him.

- When I complain about his gracious provision instead of thanking him for it, I have despised him.

This world will always have its challenges and enticements, but we must learn to value God and the things of God more. Then we will remain wholeheartedly committed to him and walk by faith. If, instead, we value ourselves and the pleasures of this world, we will always falter in our faith. It is all about what we value.

Day 48
Living without Scheming

But Jacob said, "First sell me your birthright."

—Genesis 25:31

One of my favorite Bible commentators, Warren Wiersbe, insightfully remarked, "Faith is living without scheming."[1] Yesterday, we discussed how Esau sold his birthright because he did not value it. Equally surprising, however, is Jacob's deceit in trying to obtain the birthright. Jacob was the younger son, but he was also the son of promise. God had already promised that the older son, Esau, would serve the younger son, Jacob. Yet Jacob resorted to deceit and trickery to obtain the birthright. Knowing his brother's temperament, Jacob exploited it by selling him the stew. With earthly methods, he tried to achieve God's promises. Hmmm, are we ever guilty of this? Surely Jacob forgot that the ends do not justify the means and that God will not turn a blind eye as we manipulate and deceive to receive what we want, even when what we want is a godly thing or promise.

No one will ever take from us what God has truly ordained to give us. We do not have to manipulate, scheme, and jockey for position in this world. Our position is held securely in our Lord's loving hands, and no one—I repeat, *no one*—in this world will ever take it from us. If the Lord has determined to give us something, then we will receive it. If we do not receive it, then it is not in our best interest from an eternal perspective; the "blessing" we so desperately want would turn out to be a burden. We have to stop manipulating to get what we want. For instance, at work, do we accept blame for our mistakes or try to save ourselves by shifting blame to a coworker? Do we slant the truth as we are talking to our spouse to obtain what we want? Do we manipulate and flatter people to get what we want? We do not need to exploit others' weaknesses to advance our own causes. We can trust God and rest in his sovereignty.

Day 49
Being Willing to Risk

And he said, "Come!" And Peter got out of the boat, and walked on the water and came toward Jesus.

—Matthew 14:29

In Scripture, I love the story of Peter walking on water. It had been a long night for the disciples as they sat in a boat. A storm raged around them, and then Jesus approached them, looking more like a ghost than a man. Peter cried out for Jesus to call for him, and then…Peter walked on water. Wow! Can you imagine the feeling of defying gravity and walking on water? You know what amazes me? Twelve men sat in that boat, but only one knew the exhilaration of walking on water.

If we want to experience the unimaginable in our lives, we have to be willing to risk. You know the saying "No risk, no reward. No guts, no glory." When Paul preached, he desired to preach where no one else had gone. Ruth chose to go with her mother-in-law, Naomi, and live in poverty as a widow. Peter, James, John, and Andrew walked away from their lives as fishermen and the lives they had always known to become Jesus's disciples. These were risky choices, but risk often brings the greatest reward from God.

We must be willing to leave the known for the unknown, the familiar for the unfamiliar. God may not call all of us to serve as missionaries or ministers, but he does call of us to trust him and move beyond our comfortable and secure worlds. Perhaps he wants us to share the gospel with a neighbor, take our child's friend to church, teach through a prison ministry, work with the disabled, or help inner city youth. Whatever the area, God calls us to trust him and make a difference wherever we are. Martin Luther said, "Faith is a living, daring confidence in God's grace."

Do we really want to live safe, comfortable lives and miss the glory of God? When was the last time we risked it all for him?

Day 50
Prevailing in Prayer

So I say to you, ask, and it will be given to you; seek, and you will find; knock, and it will be opened to you.

—*Luke 11:9*

In Luke 11, Jesus encouraged us to persevere in prayer by sharing a parable about a man who needed bread for a guest on a long journey. The man, realizing he had no food to offer his guest, hurried to his neighbor's house; but it was midnight, and the neighbor had already retired for the night. Initially, the neighbor declined to help the man. Yet the man persisted until the neighbor caved in and provided him bread, even though it was midnight. The Greek word used here for persistence, *anaideia*, means "recklessness, audacity, shamelessness, insolence."[1] The man shamelessly asked his neighbor for bread until the neighbor provided it. He was tenacious and persistent. As we pray, we are to pray boldly, approaching the throne of grace with confidence. There is no need that we cannot bring to the Lord.

In this parable, Jesus was not comparing God to an angry neighbor but rather contrasting the two. God is not some reluctant, irritated neighbor. He is our loving Father waiting to grant our petitions if we are his child and ask in his will. If an irritated neighbor is moved to answer a request, how much more will our loving Father answer us? As our wise and loving father, God knows exactly what we need. He knows which gifts encourage us and which gifts cause us to stumble. In the end, he wisely and generously provides us those things that we need and that help us mature.

Jesus further encouraged us to pray persistently by saying, "So I say to you, ask, and it will be given to you; seek, and you will find; knock, and it will be opened to you. For everyone who asks, receives; and he who seeks, finds; and to him who knocks, it will be opened" (Luke 11:9–10). Did you notice that each command requires progressively more action and increases in intensity? Ask requires the simple use of our voice. Seek entails more action, an earnest search. Knock demands the greatest action. It requires perseverance and great involvement on our parts. It would be a shame if we almost received an answer to prayer but gave up praying due to weariness and frustration. In order to be victorious in prayer, we must persevere in it.

Day 51
Humble before Others

Do nothing from selfishness or empty conceit, but with humility of mind regard one another as more important than yourselves.

—Philippians 2:3

Philippians 2:3 encourages us to consider others better than ourselves. This can be a challenge given our current society, which constantly focuses on ourselves, our wants, and our desires. Yet Paul admonished us to express concern for each other and to do nothing out of selfish ambition or vain conceit. Jesus repeatedly warned us that the last would be first and the first would be last. Do we truly believe him? If so, then as we perform our daily activities, are we allowing others before us or are we more concerned about ourselves and having our way?

We desperately need humility in our relationships with others. Humility enables us to apologize when we are wrong and to accept other people's apologies when they are wrong. Humility empowers us to patiently listen to others as they talk because we realize that what they have to say takes precedence over what we have to say. Humility allows us to encourage others and to build them up, instead of criticizing and tearing them down. Humility enables us to forgive others and to demonstrate mercy to those who hurt us because we realize how much we have been forgiven. Humility before others also means that we rejoice as others are blessed even if it results in a personal cost to ourselves. For instance, are we excited when a coworker receives the job promotion that we desire? Do we rejoice when another couple receives the financial blessing that we seek?

Our humility toward others is really a reflection of our humility before the Lord. Our relationship with the Lord permeates who we are, impacting all aspects of our lives, including our interactions with others. A person with a humble spirit before the Lord will also exercise a humble spirit before others. Colossians 3:12 reminds us, "So, as those who have been chosen of God, holy and beloved, put on a heart of compassion, kindness, humility, gentleness and patience." Are we clothed with humility? Does humility dominate our interactions with others?

Day 52
Shipwrecking Our Faith

Sin is crouching at the door; and its desire is for you, but you must master it.

—Genesis 4:7b

There is nothing that will shipwreck our faith more than sin. When we allow known sin into our lives, Satan uses it mercilessly to oppress us and keep us from our Lord. We must settle all scores with God, including our secret sins and our pet sins (those sins with which we have become comfortable). A little crack in a dam, for example, can remain hidden for months and even years. Over time, however, the crack grows and eventually destroys the entire dam. And so it is with us. Sin may seem insignificant, but it will completely ruin us.

Knowing the tantalizing power of sin, God warns us against it. In Genesis 4, Cain and Abel both brought the Lord an offering, but the Lord rejected Cain's offering because he did not come in faith (Heb. 11:4). Upon discovering God's displeasure, Cain felt anger and resentment. The Lord warned Cain that sin was crouching at his door; it desired to have him, but he had to master it. Unfortunately, Cain failed to take heed of God's warning, and he ended up killing his brother. Sin is so destructive, always leaving a path of devastation. We must take sin seriously and realize how truly powerful it is. Too often, we forget the transitory nature of the pleasure of sin; so let us ingrain this in our hearts: sin's pleasures are passing, temporary, short-lived. In a moment, the sweet indulgence has passed, and we are left with nothing but the devastating cost.

We must not succumb to Satan's deceitful whispers that sin is some small thing. It is not. It will completely wreck our lives, leaving us devastated and defeated. Sin is crouching at our doors; it desires to master us. We must control it through the power of God or it will shipwreck our faith. In our salvation, God did not simply save us from the penalty of sin; he also saved us from the power of sin. We *can* overcome sin through the power of God. He who is in us is greater than he who is in the world!

Day 53
Making Wise Choices

'Everything is permissible'–but not everything is beneficial. 'Everything is permissible'–but not everything is constructive.

—*1 Corinthians 10:23 (NIV)*

Life involves a series of choices that usually span the continuum from bad to okay to good to excellent. Since life provides such a variety of options for us and we live in a culture that provides an endless number of distractions, we must be wise in the choices we make. Sometimes our choices involve a good versus bad option; for instance, remaining faithful in marriage or having an affair. At other times, our choices are between two seemingly good options. These are the more difficult choices in life for we are easily swayed to settle for the good instead of striving for the excellent. Yet, we must learn to discern the better choice and to act upon it. There are times, for instance, when we may have an hour to ourselves. Do we choose to spend our time with the Lord reading the Bible or do we watch television? Neither choice is inherently bad, but we must discern the better choice. We must always choose that which has greater eternal value. If we are not careful, good can easily become the enemy of great in our lives.

First Corinthians 10:23 reminds us that though some things are permissible in our lives, they are not always beneficial to our walk of faith. In fact, even good things, if taken to the extreme, can end up hindering our faith. For example, serving at church is a commendable thing; but if I do it at the expense of prayer and daily time with the Lord, it may no longer be a good thing. We want to make choices that build us up and promote growth and maturity in our Christian walk. Our choices should bring us closer to the Lord, not draw us away.

As we seek to make excellent choices, perhaps we need to start asking ourselves the hard questions: *Does this help or hinder my walk of faith? Does this bring me closer to God or lead me away from him? Does this activity magnify God to the world?* In this life, God has offered us the excellent; let us not settle for the okay or even the good.

Day 54
Trusting God Completely

Trust in the Lord with all your heart and do not lean on your own understanding. In all your ways acknowledge him, and he will make your paths straight.

—*Proverbs 3:5–6*

Trust is essential in our relationship with the Lord and in our walk of faith. Sometimes the Lord asks what seems impossible and commands what seems unreasonable, but we are to trust him anyway. Too often, we trust in ourselves, our wisdom, our knowledge, our wealth, or our capabilities. Sometimes we trust the Lord, but only partially, keeping a backup plan in case the Lord does not come through for us. But the question before us is simple: Do we trust God? In the good times and in the bad? On the mountain tops and in the valley bottoms?

Proverbs 3:5–6 reminds us to trust the Lord with all our heart and lean not on our own understanding. If we are honest, we would probably rewrite Proverbs 3:5–6 to say, "I will trust in the Lord after exhausting other options. I will acknowledge him in some of my ways and lean on him only when absolutely necessary." Are you leaning on something besides God? It will let you down in the end. God is the only one we can lean on that will not disappoint. Only he has the strength to carry the burdens and challenges of our lives.

In our lives, we sometimes believe God is enough for salvation but is not enough for our daily living. Seems ironic, doesn't it? We trust the Lord with something as precious and serious as our eternal future, but we cannot trust him in our daily lives. And yet, we can trust God. He is absolutely faithful. He will never leave us nor forsake us. Let's decide today that no matter the circumstance, we will trust God with *all* our hearts. We will *not* lean on our own understanding, and we *will* acknowledge him in all our ways.

Day 55
Releasing Our Rights

I have been crucified with Christ; and it is no longer I who live, but Christ lives in me; and the life which I now live in the flesh I live by faith in the Son of God, who loved me and gave himself up for me.

—Galatians 2:20

To mature in our walk of faith, we have to willingly surrender our rights. It is only in releasing our rights that we experience the presence of God and the great freedom and joy that he brings.

Instead of willingly surrendering our rights, however, many times we cling to them. We may even manipulate or scheme to keep things or to maintain our way of life. And oftentimes, when we feel one of our rights is threatened, we tend to react quickly to protect it. What we hold tightly other than the Lord, we will often lose; and the more we cling to it, the greater the loss we will experience. King Saul provides a perfect example. The Lord warned him that he would lose the throne because of repeated disobedience and sin. Rather than humbly accepting the Lord's will and repenting, Saul hunted his successor David for years, even trying to kill him. During this time, Saul's greatest loss was not the loss of his throne but the loss of his precious relationship with the Lord. The more we cling to earthly rights, possessions, titles, and comforts, the greater they will corrupt us and keep us from the Lord. As Christians living and loving the Lord, we have voluntarily surrendered all rights. We have laid them at the foot of the cross. Is there a right to which you are currently clinging? The right to material possessions, the right to comfort, the right to health , the right to equal treatment, the right to instant answers, the right to be free of suffering, the right to have life your way? Jesus surrendered many of his rights when he chose to become our Savior. What right is so great that we cannot willingly surrender it for him?

It is not easy to relinquish our rights, is it? We cannot do it in our own strength. More often than not, we will choose ourselves and our rights. So let us pray and ask the Lord for help. With God's help, there is nothing we cannot do.

Day 56
Refusing to Settle for Mediocrity

I press on toward the goal for the prize of the upward call of God in Christ Jesus.

—Philippians 3:14

Our daughter Hannah is an avid soccer player. She loves the sport and plays year-round. This season, we moved her from a recreational team to a competitive team so that she could be challenged in her soccer playing and refine her skills. As you can imagine, it was quite a transition, especially since many of the girls from her new team had already played competitively. Hannah had to develop a rapport with her new teammates, learn new drills, and play on a bigger field. Her first practice game did not go well, and her coach gave her some pointers for the second game (they were playing back to back games in a hundred-degree heat). With resolve and determination, she went out and excelled in her second game. She refused to settle for okay. She refused to be simply mediocre.

In our walk of faith, there is a great temptation to become complacent and settle for mediocrity. We can easily become comfortable with the status quo, but complacency is dangerous. Have you become complacent in your walk of faith? Can you think of any ways that you have settled for mediocrity instead of pursuing the excellent? We rarely settle for mediocrity in other areas of our lives, so let us not settle in our spiritual lives. For instance, in our careers, we work hard to advance and receive promotions. In a restaurant, we expect good service and often complain when the service takes too long. Have you ever heard of a successful company who has as its slogan "Company XYZ – seeking to provide you mediocre service"? No, companies strive for excellence; and we, as Christians, should be no different.

Isaac D'Israeli insightfully remarked, "It is a wretched taste to be gratified with mediocrity when the excellent lies before us."[1] When we settle for the mediocre, we miss some of God's greatest blessings. Let us not settle for the okay when excellence beckons us!

Day 57
Our True Inheritance

Then the Lord said to Aaron, "You shall have no inheritance in their land nor own any portion among them; I am your portion and your inheritance among the sons of Israel."

—Numbers 18:20

After spending forty years in the desert for their unbelief, the twelve tribes of Israel finally entered Canaan, the promised land.

One of these tribes, the tribe of Levi, was considered the priestly tribe. As Israel entered the promised land, the Lord allocated land as an inheritance to all the different tribes, except the tribe of Levi. Why? The Lord was to be their inheritance (Num. 18:20–21, Deut. 14:27). A. W. Tozer insightfully commented, "God said to him [the Levites] simply, 'I am thy part and thine inheritance,' and by those words made him richer than all his brethren, richer than all the kings and rajas who have ever lived in the world. And there is a spiritual principle here, a principle still valid for every priest of the Most High God. The man who has God for His treasure has all things in One."[1]

I imagine that some of the people from the other tribes might have felt a little sorry for the Levites because they did not receive any land as their inheritance. But the Levites had received the greatest inheritance ever—not something earthly and passing like land, but something eternal and lasting, the Lord Himself. The priests could not have asked for a more precious inheritance than the one they had received. If we lived during those times and were a priest, would we be disappointed that we had not received land? Would we understand that the Lord is all the inheritance we ever need? Our inheritance is not comprised of our transitory, material possessions, such as a house, car, or money. It is the Lord Himself. We should not be seeking the things of God but God Himself, for He is our true inheritance. He is our portion. He is our very great reward. So let us ask the Lord to help us to love Him deeply and passionately. Let us cry out to Him to show us the depth of his riches and to display His magnificence to us.

Day 58
Weak Yet Truly Strong

And he has said to me, "My grace is sufficient for you, for power is perfected in weakness." Most gladly, therefore, I will rather boast about my weaknesses, so that the power of Christ may dwell in me.

—*2 Corinthians 12:9*

Second Corinthians 12:9 is a favorite verse for many Christians. And yet, when we apply it to our lives, it is not quite that simple or easy. For the Israelites, for instance, it meant being sandwiched between the Egyptian army and the Red Sea, two terrifying options. But then God parted the Red Sea and beautifully displayed his glory. For us, it usually means that we are in places of weakness and difficulty. But who of us likes to be in places of weakness? We would prefer to be strong and in control. When we finally exhaust all human options, however, God steps in and reveals his glory, and we stand amazed by such beauty!

In those places of weakness, however, 2 Corinthians 12:9–10 quietly reminds us " 'My grace is sufficient for you, for power is perfected in weakness.' Most gladly, therefore, I will rather boast about my weaknesses, so that the power of Christ may dwell in me. Therefore I am well content with weaknesses, with insults, with distresses, with persecutions, with difficulties, for Christ's sake; for when I am weak, then I am strong." In these verses, Paul said that the Lord's power is made perfect in our weaknesses, not in our strengths; in our flaws, not in our perfections. In our strengths and perfections, people are tempted to give us honor and praise, honor and praise that rightfully belong to the Lord. Thus, the Lord uses our weaknesses and infirmities so that people will know from where the true power comes.

Now let's be honest. As soon as difficulties enter our lives, we usually pray and plead that the Lord will remove them. Instead, the Lord whispers, "I am glorified most in your weakness, not your strength." Never let your weakness hinder you for it can beautifully reveal God's strength. God used a stone to kill a giant, Moses's rod to give Israel victory, and a little boy's lunch to feed the thousands. When we are weak, then we are truly strong, so let's make sure we turn our weaknesses over to God!

Day 59
Overcoming Fear

For God has not given us a spirit of timidity, but of power and love and discipline.

—*2 Timothy 1:7*

Fear of flying. Fear of heights. Fear of loneliness. Fear of betrayal. Fear of failure. Fear of rejection. Fear of disease. Fear of death. There it is—fear, lurking around every corner, seeking to consume us, waiting to dismantle our faith. It steals our joy, threatens our peace, and enslaves us mercilessly. Without a doubt, fear is one of Satan's greatest tools against us, and he wields it with remarkable precision. If he can keep us beholden to fear, we will not fulfill God's calling for our lives. Fear can shape our whole lives and keep us from acting in faith.

Once fear begins to rise in us, we must stop it immediately or it will build and grow. Our imagination will magnify the fear, laying out a thousand horrible possibilities. The small molehill soon becomes a mountain, and before we know it, our fears have overcome our faith. Second Timothy 1:7 reminds us that God has not given us a spirit of fear but of power and love. Fear characterized our lives before Christ when we feared what other men feared. Now we know the greatness of our God, and he is so much greater than our worst fear. He can help us overcome every fear we face. Our fears will always seem great until we place them in perspective with God. For example, when I stand at street-level and see a skyscraper, it looks enormous to me, but when I fly in a plane, that same skyscraper seems quite small. It is about perspective. God is greater than anything we face, so let us rest in his greatness.

No matter what we face, we can always take refuge in God because he will protect us, provide for us, and care for us. When we find ourselves succumbing to fear, let us focus on God and cry out to him through prayer. Scripture repeatedly calls us to act in faith, but too often, we allow our fears to overcome our faith. What if instead our faith overcame our fear? Can you imagine the possibilities of living a fearless life? Can you imagine what God could do through a fearless person?

Day 60
Remembering God's
Past Faithfulness

Each of you take up a stone on his shoulder, according to the number of the tribes of the sons of Israel. Let this be a sign among you.

—*Joshua 4:5b–6a*

In the Old Testament, God required the Israelites to celebrate several main feasts each year. The feasts comprised a total of seventy days or 19 percent of the year.[1] Their main purpose was to remember God and his great faithfulness. Why would God require the Israelites to spend 19 percent of their year in celebration and remembrance? Because he knows how short our memories are; he knows how quickly we can forget his provision and goodness. And yet, remembering God's past faithfulness helps us trust God more in the present. This is why the Lord repeatedly reminded the Israelites to remember his workings and to not forget him. For instance, when the Israelites crossed the

Jordan River to enter the promised land, the Lord instructed them to build a memorial to him out of twelve stones (Josh. 4:1–7). In future generations, when the children asked the purpose of the stones, the Israelites were to remind their children of the Lord and his faithfulness.

We too need to establish memorials in our lives, places where we remember the Lord's goodness and graciousness to us. Perhaps we can keep a journal chronicling God's great acts. Perhaps we can create a photo collage of certain events. Perhaps we can make certain holidays, like Thanksgiving, times of remembrance. Somehow, we need to remember how God has lovingly been there for us in the past. One of my greatest trials occurred in my first pregnancy when I was pregnant with our twin boys. It was a high-risk, life-threatening pregnancy fraught with difficulties and challenges; and yet, in many ways, that challenging season helped to cement my relationship of faith. I can remember God's strength when I was tired, his love when I was lonely from being on bed rest, and his comfort when we were told one of our children was going to die. Whenever I struggle in my faith, I can return to this time to see God's past faithfulness; this helps remind me of God's current faithfulness to me even when the situation seems bleak and overwhelming. God's past faithfulness always points to his future faithfulness.

Day 61
The Snare of Man

The fear of man brings a snare, but he who trusts in the Lord will be exalted.

—Proverbs 29:25

Proverbs 29:25 reminds us that the fear of man will prove to be a snare. The Hebrew word for snare means "the lure or bait placed in a hunter's trap."[1] If we are honest, the fear of man, which involves worrying about what people think of us, is a hard thing to resist, and it subtly lures us into its trap. Even some of God's greatest men struggled with the fear of man. For example, in Genesis 12, there was a famine in Canaan, so Abraham left the promised land and traveled to Egypt, where there was food. Because Sarah, his wife, was a beautiful woman, Abraham feared that Pharaoh would kill him and take Sarah as his wife, so he told Sarah to lie and say she was his sister. The fear of man causes us to act irrationally, doesn't it? It also may cause us to lie or commit additional sins. Worst of all, our fear of man ruins our witness for God. Pharaoh's household discovered Abraham's duplicity; and in the end, Pharaoh, a nonbeliever, showed more character than Abraham, God's own man.

Though the fear of man ensnares us, trusting in God results in our exaltation. The Hebrew word for exaltation, *sagab*, means "to be raised, to be exalted, to be high, to

111

defend."[2] What a beautiful contrast to when we fear man, so let's choose to trust in God instead.

Remembering the greatness of God also helps us to not fear man. When we stand in awe of who God is, we will care less what man thinks of us. Sometimes we just need a gentle reminder of how truly magnificent our Lord is—he who made the heavens, who laid the foundation of the earth, who formed man, who made the sun stand still, who parted the waters, who flooded the earth, who upholds the universe. Why do we fear man when before us stands *Almighty God?* In the end, everything in this world will fade away. The greatest empires will crumble, the most powerful rulers will die, buildings will be destroyed, lands will be ravaged, but God will endure forever. Surely history is the greatest evidence that no one will outlive, outmaneuver, outpower, outsmart, or outwit God. He remains forever. He is the great I AM.

Day 62
Acting with Selflessness

Turn my heart toward your statutes and not toward selfish gain.

—*Psalm 119:36 (NIV)*

Walking in faith means choosing to act selflessly and placing others before ourselves. In Scripture, a man named

Jonathan beautifully displays this selflessness. He was the eldest son of King Saul and a courageous warrior. He was also a man devoted to God and willing to do God's will no matter the personal cost (1 Sam. 14:1–15). Over the course of his life, Jonathan became the best friend of David, the second king of Israel and King Saul's successor. This friendship would reveal Jonathan's love for his Lord and his selflessness. Imagine for a moment, that you are Jonathan. Your father is the current king of Israel, and you think you will inherit the throne. Now imagine that a competitor, David, has arisen from the ashes and will probably take the throne. What would you do? Would you befriend him or seek his ruin? Remember you have probably been schooled into believing that you would succeed your father as king. Would you scheme and manipulate to secure the throne or would you humbly acknowledge God's will and help your challenger? This was the situation that Jonathan faced, and yet he responded with remarkable faith in God and exhibited great selflessness.

Despite his situation, Jonathan chose to cultivate his friendship with David. He went even further by pledging to help David secure the throne at personal risk to himself. Jonathan could have easily allowed his father to kill David, thereby securing the throne for himself. He could have easily given in to selfish ambition and caused unnecessary fighting with David and the people. Instead, Jonathan helped David and willingly placed aside any personal dreams he had by performing God's will.

In our walk of faith, God asks us to demonstrate selflessness. We will have to step away from things to which we feel entitled. Are we willing to surrender our personal ambitions, money, comfort, and earthly belongings for someone else? Will we selflessly walk away from a position to which we feel "entitled"? These are hard questions, aren't they? So let's ask the Lord to turn our hearts toward his statutes and not toward selfish gain (Ps. 119:36).

Day 63
Strengthened by the Holy Spirit

> *In the same way the Spirit also helps our weakness; for we do not know how to pray as we should, but the Spirit Himself intercedes for us with groanings too deep for words; and he who searches the hearts knows what the mind of the Spirit is, because he intercedes for the saints according to the will of God.*
>
> *—Romans 8:26–27*

Romans 8:26–27 provides great encouragement to us. Who of us has never struggled with prayer before? Sometimes the words just do not seem to come. We sit lost in our thoughts, so overwhelmed with circumstances that we do not know what to pray for. But the Holy Spirit understands our situation, and he helps us. What comfort to know that we have someone praying for us, even when we least expect it. When I first started teaching, God raised up a total stranger to pray for me. The man saw me in church and felt led to pray for me. I felt thrilled to know that the Lord had raised someone up to pray for me. That is what the Holy Spirit does for us *daily*. Isn't that exciting!

Since the Holy Spirit searches our hearts and knows our minds, he knows where we struggle and can intercede perfectly for us through prayer. The Greek word for intercede is a "picturesque word of rescue by one who 'happens on' (*entugcanei*) one who is in trouble and 'in his behalf' (*huper*) pleads 'with unuttered groanings.'"[1] That is an interesting description, isn't it? In essence, it means to rescue someone who is in trouble but has no resources.

The Holy Spirit also knows God's perfect will for us. Since we see everything through such a limited view, it can make it difficult to discern God's will. The Holy Spirit, however, knows God's will and can make perfect intercession for us, praying for God's will for our lives and for our eternal best. Through the Holy Spirit, God encourages us in our maturity and helps us to reach our full potential.

Day 64
Ensnared by Envy

A heart at peace gives life to the body, but envy rots the bones.

—*Proverbs 14:30 (NIV)*

Someone has said that envy is the sin of the have-nots against the haves. *Vines Dictionary* defines envy as "the feeling of displeasure produced by witnessing or hearing of the advantage or prosperity of others."[1] Envy desires what someone else has or wishes the other person had it to a lesser degree. In its advanced state, it can actually seek the ruin of the person and take pleasure in his failure. For example, it may bother us when someone else purchases the bigger house we wanted or when a coworker receives the job promotion we feel we deserved. We may feel vindicated or even happy when the person is later fired or loses the house.

Proverbs 14:30 reminds us that envy rots the bones. It eats away at our soul. Envy subtly begins to affect our thinking, demeanor, and relationships with others. It also incites other sins, like anger, adultery, theft, quarrels, fights, violence, and murder. Envy is a quiet but powerful vice that Satan skillfully uses to cripple our walk of faith and our ability to witness to others. After all, how can we witness to the unsaved when we lie consumed with envy of what they have? How can we honestly tell people that Jesus is the answer, that he is all they need, when we desire more than just him?

To overcome envy, we need to recognize that envy is sin and confess it to the Lord. We also need to pray for ourselves that God will help us find contentment in his current provision. Envy is not really about us and the other person; it is about us and God. We resent that God chose to give someone else what we desire, so we must turn back to God and rest in his provision for us. God knows exactly what we need and when we need it. We must stop envying what others have or it will emotionally and spiritually exhaust us. And really, we do not need to envy others for we each have true riches—the Lord Himself. He is greater than any possession or comfort this world can ever offer us.

Day 65
Walking by Faith

For we walk by faith, not by sight.

—*2 Corinthians 5:7*

Second Corinthians 5:7 beautifully captures the essence of the Christian walk: we are to live and walk by faith, not by the law, not by legalism, not by circumstance, not by logic, and not by feelings. Sometimes, if we are honest, our

Christian walk is based more on our feelings than on our faith. The problem, however, is that our feelings can easily deceive us. That is not to say that our emotions and feelings are always wrong; they are not, for God gave us emotions, but sometimes they lead us astray and must be submitted to the Word of God. For instance, during a hardship, our feelings may tell us that God does not love us, and yet the Word of God tells us that God sent his only Son to redeem us because of his great love for us. We must learn to walk by our will and not by our emotions or we will get sidetracked in our walk of faith.

Second Corinthians 5:7 also reminds us to not walk by sight. Truth be told, our sight is one of the great hindrances to our walk of faith because we choose to trust only in what we know and see; but things are not always how we see them. Second Kings 6 tells the interesting story of how the Arameans devised a plot to capture the prophet Elisha. They sent hundreds of horses, chariots, and men to surround him. When Elisha's servant saw the great army, fear and dread overcame him. Elisha, however, said the most interesting thing, "'O Lord, I pray, open his eyes that he may see.' And the Lord opened the servant's eyes and he saw; and behold, the mountain was full of horses and chariots of fire all around Elisha" (2 Kings 6:17). God had an army of horses and chariots surrounding Elisha and his servant to protect them. Then

God struck down the Arameans' army with blindness, and Elisha emerged the victor against thousands of men. Behind the physical realities we see lie spiritual realities we do not see. We must trust God and choose to walk by faith, even when things go dark. Then we will see the glory of God shine through!

Day 66
Approaching the Throne of Grace

Therefore let us draw near with confidence to the throne of grace, so that we may receive mercy and find grace to help in time of need.

—Hebrews 4:16

In our walk of faith, God's grace is there for us, and it is there in abundance to help us overcome the challenges and difficulties of this life and to bring glory to his name. So what is grace? Someone once said that grace is "God's Riches At Christ's Expense." The Greek word for grace, *charis*, means the "unmerited favor of God." Grace is kindness and compassion extended to those who do not deserve it and who could never earn it. Grace is based completely on the giver and does not depend on the recipient. It is never earned, deserved, or merited.

Though we have experienced God's grace from the moment of our births, the greatest manifestation occurred in our salvation when we were saved by grace (Eph. 2:8–9). But God's grace does not end with our salvation; it continues on in our lives as redeemed children of God. God gives us grace for everyday living, grace for trials, grace for service, grace for our worst mistakes, grace to be the people God desires us to be.

In our walk of faith, if we rely on our own strength and power, we will fail miserably and, worse yet, become discouraged and disillusioned. We cannot rely on pure grit and determination alone; we desperately need grace. God makes that grace readily accessible to each of us. "Therefore let us draw near with confidence to the throne of grace, so that we may receive mercy and find grace to help in time of need" (Heb. 4:16). Hebrews 4:16 paints such a beautiful visual. It calls God's throne the *throne of grace*. Not the throne of judgment, not the throne of wrath, but the throne of grace—a throne in which God has poured out his love and compassion. We stand and walk in grace—abundant, overflowing grace. No matter what we face, God has the right amount of grace for us. It is sufficient to deal with difficult, wearisome people. It is sufficient to deal with trying circumstances. It is sufficient to hold our tongues when we would rather speak unkindly. It is sufficient to forgive what seems unforgiveable. It is sufficient for *all* our needs.

Day 67
Remaining Faithful to the Vision

Where there is no vision, the people are unrestrained.

—Proverbs 29:18a

Several years ago, I had the privilege of going on a mission trip to Estonia. Most of our work involved handing out Christian tracts, but we were also given the opportunity to talk to some female inmates in an Estonian prison. When I first heard about the opportunity, I was filled with enthusiasm. How exciting to share God with these women. Then a funny thing happened. As I shared with my Christian friends, they asked questions like, "Is it safe? Do their guards carry guns? What about a lockdown? What about disease?" So I did the natural thing: I googled answers to my questions. The answers were not very reassuring, but I decided that if God had called me to do this, I would go and not be swayed by other's opinions. And I tell you what—it was absolutely amazing! The female inmates were overwhelmed with the fact that we had taken time out of our busy schedules to share the love of Christ with them. It was the highlight of my trip, a high of highs.

When God gives us a vision to do something, we must be faithful to it or we will miss untold blessings. What joy I would have missed had I not met these women. God has certain things that he wants each of us to accomplish in our lives to bring him glory, and we have to be willing to obey him. Let me also clarify that as God calls us to act, it is never contrary to his Word. He, who gave us his Word, would never act against its truth or beauty. Thus, God would never "call" us to commit adultery because we are in a bad marriage or steal from our jobs because we need money; that is our own sinful desires overcoming us.

It is not always easy to act on the vision that God gives us, but we must try and remain faithful to it. With my Estonian trip, I realized too that God does not always give others the vision that he gives us so they sometimes see the negatives of the situation. God does not give them the grace because they are not the ones being called to obey. We are each responsible for obedience to the vision that God gives. Let us be found faithful!

Day 68
Staying Alert and Self-Controlled

Be of sober spirit, be on the alert. Your adversary, the devil, prowls around like a roaring lion, seeking someone to devour.

—*1 Peter 5:8*

We are in a spiritual war, and we have a real adversary: Satan. His intention is our complete destruction, and he is on the offensive. That sounds ominous, doesn't it? First Peter 5:8

tells us that Satan continually looks for someone to devour. It is hard to imagine someone hating us so much that they would vindictively try to hurt us. Truth be told, most of us do not imagine the devil as seeking to fully destroy us. But Satan hates God that much, and since we are God's prized possession, he hates us as well. We should never think that Satan cares for us or that he has any compassion; he does not. There is a reason Peter compared Satan to a roaring lion and not to a quiet mouse. Lions are vicious and brutal. They stealthily stalk their prey until the right time; then they pounce on their victim without warning. Satan continually prowls the earth, seeking victims that he may devour. He wants to destroy our fellowship with God, ruin our witness to others, and steal our peace and joy.

Because Satan is a strong enemy, 1 Peter 5:8 commands us to remain sober and alert so that we do not succumb to Satan's temptations. What often happens, however, is that we lower our guard. As soon as Satan sees that, he sweeps in for the kill, launching a full onslaught against us. Once we sin, we also provide Satan the opportunity to create a stronghold in our lives. The more times we sin in an area, the greater the risk of a stronghold. Once a stronghold has been created, Satan will not release it without an enormous fight. Can you think of any sins that have become strongholds? If you are unsure, try keeping a spiritual diary, noting the types of sins to which you succumb. Do some sins frequently seem to gain victory over you? Then try and place the necessary guards in your life to prevent those types of sins.

Day 69
Moving Past Our Failures

And he [Jesus] came the third time, and said to them, "Are you still sleeping and resting? It is enough; the hour has come; behold, the Son of Man is being betrayed into the hands of sinners."

—*Mark 14:41*

Someone once said that the Christian walk is a series of new beginnings. I love that! At some point in our walk of faith, we all need to start fresh, to leave our past baggage at the foot of the cross—all those past mistakes, past failures, past sins.

In Mark 14:41, Jesus and some of his disciples (James, John, and Peter) entered the Garden of Gethsemane. Jesus's time to be crucified had arrived, so he spent hours in sweet communion praying to the Father. Before leaving the disciples, he told them to keep watch. A little later, he returned and found all three of them asleep. He reminded them again to keep watching and praying. He returned a second and a third time only to find them asleep. Can you imagine? At this point, the disciples had walked with Jesus for almost three years, yet they failed him. One simple command: stay awake and pray. Three opportunities to prove faithful, three failures in a row, at one of Jesus's most important times. If the disciples better understood what Jesus was about to endure, perhaps they would have been more diligent in staying awake and praying. But that is why we walk by faith and not by sight. God does not always explain things to us in advance. The disciples missed sharing a sacred moment with Jesus because they fell asleep.

Amazingly, Jesus chose to forgive Peter, James, and John for their failing and mistake. In our walk of faith, God does not expect perfection from us, just sincerity and a willingness to be changed for his glory. We are all growing and maturing in our faith. At times, we still succumb to sin, and we still fail God. God's call to a life of faith could easily overwhelm us if we do not realize that God leads us one day at a time. Little by little, he changes us and conforms us to Christ, moving us from glory to greater glory.

Day 70
Leaving the Saltshaker

You are the salt of the earth.

—Matthew 5:13a

In Matthew 5:13, Jesus said that believers are the salt of the earth. Notice that Jesus did not say that we "should be" the salt; he simply said you "are" the salt. Being the salt is an amazing privilege! We are meant to bless the world around us. In ancient times, salt was invaluable to society, just as we, as Christians, are invaluable to the society in which we live.

Salt has the ability to hinder corruption and to serve as a preservative, thereby keeping food from spoiling. We serve as salt by preserving purity and hindering wickedness in the world. This means standing up for the Lord and obeying his commands, regardless of the cost. It means being different because we will not tolerate sin. It means that we may not say or do things that this world considers "normal" because they offend the Lord. Are we serving as a preservative by taking a stand for God?

Salt also has a healing effect. In ancient times, salt was used to heal open wounds. When salt made initial contact, however, it stung; but afterward, it had an amazing healing and renewing quality. This is also true for us. When we act as salt and share God's truth with others, it may initially sting and burn, but we still have to share it. Jesus did not call us the "honey of the earth." Sometimes, we want to sugarcoat everything, not wanting to offend anyone or hurt anyone's feelings. We rationalize that we might offend someone, but in doing so, we fail to be the salt that Jesus has called us to be. Once we share God's truth, the residual effect is healing, an enhanced quality of life, and a renewed relationship with the Father.

Salt also seasons food, making it more palatable. By itself, salt does not taste very pleasing. Only in the right quantity does it transform bland food into tasty food. In order for salt to effectively season, it must come into contact with something; it must leave the saltshaker. We cannot remain in the saltshaker and expect to impact this world for Christ.

Day 71
Having a Discerning Heart

So give your servant a discerning heart to govern your people and to distinguish between right and wrong. For who is able to govern this great people of yours?

—1 Kings 3:9 (NIV)

King Solomon was the son of King David and Bathsheba. He ruled Israel as its third king for forty years around 1000 BC. One night, the Lord appeared to him in a dream, telling him to ask for whatever he wanted. If the Lord told us to ask for anything, what would we ask for? Would we ask for riches, honor, career advancement, health, friends, or family? Or would we instead ask for a heart to always love and cherish our Lord? Would we ask for temporary things or eternal ones? Don't quickly pass by this question. The things for which we ask reveal a great deal about what lies in our heart. For what *one* thing would we ask?

Solomon asked for a discerning heart to govern God's people and to distinguish between right and wrong. Discerning right from wrong can be challenging because Satan often masquerades as an angel of light to deceive us. We can frequently recognize blatant wrong, such as murder or stealing; it is the shades of gray that seem more difficult. Sometimes we confuse the two because on the surface they seem similar. It takes great discernment to see what lies hidden below the surface.

Today, discernment is vital when it comes to people who teach the Bible. Not every professed Bible teacher actually teaches the Word of God, and like the Bereans, we must examine the Scriptures and test our Bible teachers against the Word. "Now these were more noble-minded than those in Thessalonica, for they received the word with great eagerness, examining the Scriptures daily to see whether these things were so" (Acts 17:11). Imagine, the Bereans took the words of the apostle Paul, who eventually wrote one-third of the New Testament, and examined them to make sure he spoke God's truth. As long as we test others in a humble and kind spirit and not critically or self-righteously, we will strengthen the body of Christ. We have the spirit of truth in us, the Holy Spirit, and he can easily lead us into all truth if we willingly listen to him (John 14:17). The Holy Spirit will use the filter of the Word to help us discern truth from falsehood and good from evil.

Day 72
Surrendering Control to God

Father, if you are willing, remove this cup from me; yet not my will, but yours be done.

—Luke 22:42

A huge part of walking by faith means surrendering control of *all* parts of our lives to God, but surrendering control is a hard thing. Deep down, many of us want life our way and want to control the things in our lives.

One weekend in our ladies' Bible study class, one of my coteachers explained her surrendering control to God by using a car analogy. At first, Jesus was in the car with her, but he was in the backseat. Slowly over time, she gave God some control of her life and moved him to the front seat, but she still would not let him drive. Eventually, she gave him control of her life and allowed him to drive. When she said that, another lady remarked, "I have no problems with Jesus driving, as long as he takes me where I want to go." At that point, I laughed because isn't that the truth? Even with Jesus driving, I still want to go where I want and, I might add, on my timetable. If we are honest, we often want life our way with God thrown in when we need him; but that is not how God meant for us to live our lives. Have you fully surrendered to God, or are you still trying to live your life and fit God in where convenient?

Control is a hard thing to surrender, and so sometimes, we only partially surrender our lives to God. The part that we hold back, however, will wreak emotional and spiritual havoc with us every single time. It is so much better to give God control over all aspects of our lives. And when we do, we will experience incredible joy and freedom. We no longer have to worry over every detail of our lives or when plans get disrupted because we can trust God to work everything out. Is there an area of your life you need to surrender to God? To help us in this challenging area, maybe we need to start our days on our knees, telling God that we will surrender control to him for that day so that we can bring him glory.

Day 73
Persevering in Our Faith

For you have need of endurance, so that when you have done the will of God, you may receive what was promised.

—Hebrews 10:36

This life is challenging. Difficulties abound. Hardships sometimes seem to swallow us. If we are honest, there are times when we are so overwhelmed that we want to quit. Persevering in our faith is not always easy, but it is worth it. Several years ago, I had the crazy idea that I should join a friend and run a half marathon. As we started our exercise routine, it was a grueling and difficult process. My friend started getting sore ankles and bleeding feet, while I started having backaches and sore knees. At the time, it would have been easy to dwell on the pain and to give up. Instead, we chose to persevere and push through the pain. Eventually, we completed our half marathon. All the pain and suffering from the prior months were eclipsed by crossing the finish line and receiving our medals.

Knowing this journey is challenging, God encourages us to persevere in our faith. The Greek word translated as perseverance means "bearing up under, patience, endurance as to things or circumstances...that quality of character which does not allow one to surrender to circumstances or succumb under trial."[1] Perseverance is persistence, endurance, steadfastness. It is the act of continuing regardless of circumstances, hardships, or trials. Sometimes, it seems that the more we act in faith, the harder our circumstances become; but that is only from an earthly perspective. Our reward is coming. We just have to wait for it.

No matter the difficulty or hardship, God wants us to persevere. We may currently be experiencing a sowing season, but the reaping season is around the corner if we will persevere. One day, I was reading through Numbers 7, which at first glance is a long list of names. Then, it occurred to me that God had taken meticulous note of each leader's name and his offering. What a great encouragement to us that God carefully observes everything we do in faith. There is no act, no matter how small, that goes unnoticed; and truth be told, in the kingdom of God there are no small acts. Though this world and its people may never see our acts of faith, God does and he will reward us for them. Can you imagine your beloved Lord turning to you and saying, "Well done, my good and faithful servant. I am so proud of you!" So let us persevere in our faith!

Day 74
Deepening Our Faith

So faith comes from hearing, and hearing by the word of Christ.

—*Romans 10:17*

One of the greatest ways to deepen our faith is to read the Bible. Romans 10:17 reminds us that faith comes from hearing the Word of God. We cannot worship a God we do not know, and the best way to know God is to read and study his word. Reading the Bible equips us in several ways. It guides and directs us, serving as a lamp to our feet and a light for our path. It encourages us and helps build our faith. During times of trials, it strengthens and comforts us. The Word illustrates God's faithfulness in past generations so that we can apply that same faithfulness to us. It reveals God's wisdom and instruction so that we do not travel down wrong paths. The Bible teaches and trains us in righteousness so that we are equipped to do God's work. It completely revitalizes our lives of faith and transforms us.

In order to be transformed, however, we must make reading God's Word a commitment and a priority. We live in a world in which many things compete for our attention. Truth be told, we are all busy, very busy, but we must learn to focus on that which has true eternal value and will endure forever—our relationship with the Lord. Spending time with God through prayer and studying his Word must take precedence over everything else in our lives. Getting to know God should be our top priority, even if it means sacrificing our personal time, hobbies, volunteer time, or work.

This world is difficult; we face adversity on every side. The Word of God grounds, encourages, and sustains us. It provides an anchor for us, a root system on which we can draw. We desperately need the strength, encouragement, and fortitude that the Word provides. Without knowing the truths of God's Word, we will waver and doubt in our Christian faith. So let's start devoting time to Bible study today so that we can deepen our faith and live victoriously!

Day 75
Encouraging One Another

We urge you, brethren, admonish the unruly, encourage the fainthearted, help the weak, be patient with everyone.

—*1 Thessalonians 5:14*

In Scripture, there was an interesting man named Apollos, who was an eloquent speaker with a good knowledge of the Scriptures (Acts 18:24–28). When he spoke the gospel, he had great fervor and boldness, but his message lacked complete information. Priscilla and Aquila, a godly couple in the area, heard him speak and appreciated his passion and enthusiasm. They also knew that he did not completely understand salvation, so they took him quietly to their home and explained salvation more fully to him. Apollos accepted their instruction, allowed it to change him, and continued his work for the Lord. Scripture later reveals that God used Apollos in mighty ways; some people even placed him on the same level with Paul and Peter (1 Cor. 1:12).

What a great reminder to us on the importance of investing time and effort in the lives of others to encourage them in their walk of faith. In this instance, Priscilla and Aquila took time to correct Apollos because his doctrine was not complete. They could have easily continued with their daily duties, but they chose instead to make time and reveal the truth to Apollos. And what if this couple had ignored helping Apollos? He, in turn, may not have helped hundreds of other people.

God does not want us so busy in our lives that we miss opportunities to strengthen and edify others. In 1 Thessalonians 5:14, Paul mentioned several ways we can strengthen others: warn the unruly, encourage the discouraged, help the weak, and exhibit patience. We are meant to nurture and encourage each other in our walk of faith. The Christian walk can sometimes be a lonely place, and each of us desperately needs one another. Perhaps someone needs a meal because they are experiencing a difficult trial. Or perhaps someone needs a card of encouragement because they have lost a loved one. Or perhaps someone needs to be gently and lovingly rebuked. What an exciting privilege that God uses us to make a difference in the lives of others. God has meant for us to be accountable to one another and to help one another in our walk of faith.

Day 76
Moving On to Maturity

Therefore leaving the elementary teaching about the Christ, let us press on to maturity.

—*Hebrews 6:1a*

One of the greatest detriments in our walk of faith is that we are easily satisfied with a measly morsel so we lay famished when we could feast at the Master's table. If we could enjoy a scrumptious piece of chocolate cake, why would we settle for a piece of old, stale bread? And yet many of us do that every day. Rather than feasting on God's Word, we choose instead to feast on the things of this world. As a result, we lay famished and starving. Instead, let's develop an appetite for the Word and the things of God. The Word is our continual source of nourishment; it is the powerhouse of our growth. The more time we spend reading and meditating on it, the more we will stay nourished.

The writer of Hebrews rebuked some of the early Christians for still being infants. Though they should have been teachers, they still needed someone to explain the basic truths of God's Word to them. These Christians needed milk, not solid food. When a baby is born, he thrives on milk; but over time, he progresses to good, solid food. When we first became a Christian, our diet consisted of milk, and there is nothing wrong with that. But over time, it should change to good, hearty meat.

In Hebrews 6:1, we are encouraged to leave the elementary teachings about Christ and press on to maturity. Though the ABCs of Scripture were necessary as a child, we must now move on to substantial Christian teachings and doctrines. If we want to become a mathematician, for instance, we would have to move past understanding simple addition, like one plus one is two. Have we moved beyond the simple ABCs of Scripture? Are we still drinking milk or eating steak? Can we handle meat that is tougher and harder to swallow? Unless we spend time daily reading and meditating on the Word, we will still need milk. The Word of God has been compared to a raw precious stone; in order to find the jewel, we must exert the time and effort to mine and polish it. We must willingly devote ourselves to the study of the Word and prayer. We must saturate our minds with the Word of God.

Day 77
Resting in God's Faithfulness

If we are faithless, he remains faithful, for he cannot deny himself.

—*2 Timothy 2:13*

One of the greatest comforts in our faith is knowing that God is faithful to us even when we are faithless. When we falter, when we stumble, or when we just fall flat, God remains faithful to us because faithfulness is part of his very nature. "If we are faithless, he remains faithful, for he cannot deny himself" (2 Tim. 2:13). God will always help, encourage, and strengthen us. He is dependable and can be trusted to the nth degree. He will never fail nor forsake us.

One of my favorite Bible characters is Peter because of his devotion to Christ. And yet, Peter experienced more than his fair share of faithless moments. In one of those moments, he denied Christ—not once, not twice, but three times. Did God simply throw away Peter in favor of someone else? Did he refuse to use Peter in his work? No, quite the opposite. After repenting, Jesus restored Peter to service, and Peter went on to preach at Pentecost, where three thousand people were saved.

What God has started in us, he will finish! "For I am confident of this very thing, that he who began a good work in you will perfect it until the day of Christ Jesus" (Phil. 1:6). Praise God for that because I know that if it were up to me, I would be too faithless to carry on at times. Think of how you were before you accepted Christ as Lord and Savior and now look at yourself today. The Lord has done that for us. He has brought us this far, and he will continue to work in us. God provides the strength, solace, and encouragement we need. He gives us the will to go on and to be faithful in the trying times. And no matter what, he will not give up on us!

Day 78
Acting on Our Faith

I will show you my faith by my works.

—James 2:18b

Though we may spend a great deal of time talking about faith, ultimately faith is not something that we just discuss; it is something that we do. Our faith should be active, not passive. It yields actions. It yields obedience, even when obedience may be inconvenient or costly. Thus, as God calls us to do something, we must obey him. I believe; therefore, I act.

One of the interesting things about obeying God and acting in faith is that it grows our view of God. That is not to say that God is small, he is not; but too often, we have a small view of him because we fail to act when he commands us. Every time God calls us to act in faith and we obey him, it grows our view of him.

Several years ago, my ministry team decided to host a fun luncheon for the girls. At the same time, we felt led to donate one thousand of my *Reclaiming Your Joy* Bible study books to a local women's prison. Because we were a new ministry, we could not afford to pay for the books and would need donations. The night before the luncheon, I felt like God impressed on me to ask for donations at the luncheon. I have to confess, my initial reaction was "No, this is a fun girls' afternoon, and nothing will ruin that faster than asking for money." However, choosing to act in faith, I mentioned it at the end of the luncheon. Wow, there were only sixty ladies in attendance, but we received funds for almost seven hundred books! Can you imagine? My team stood shocked at what God had done, and it grew our view of God, our Great Provider. Are you ready for God to enlarge your view of him? Then get ready to act in faith!

Day 79
Strengthened by God's Discipline

For those whom the Lord loves he disciplines, and he scourges every son whom he receives.

—Hebrews 12:6

Wouldn't it be nice if every time we told our child to do something, he did it? Better yet, can you imagine a life where we never had to discipline our child because he always obeyed us? And now back to reality. The truth is our children do disobey us, and with the greatest of love, we discipline them for their own good. In our lives, God is no different; he disciplines his children because he loves them.

Hebrews 12:5–11 reminds us that discipline is a part of our Christian walk and actually strengthens our faith. The Greek word for discipline, *paideia*, relates to the training and instruction of a child and entails correction. Thus, the Lord's discipline is not some harsh retribution but rather a purposed training of us. In his discipline, God is correcting us, not rejecting us. It is important to remember that the Lord disciplines us because he loves us, just as we discipline our children because we love them. God's discipline is for our eternal good and well-being. Discipline helps us to grow and mature and become more like him. Sometimes we stray in our walk of faith, and God uses discipline to return us to the right path. He knows the sorrow and suffering we will experience if we continue down a wrong path. And God is the perfect discipliner; since he created us, he knows the exact measure of discipline that we need to correct our behavior. This is also why we never want to compare our discipline with someone else's. Some Christians are more responsive and need a milder discipline, while some of us have harder heads and need a harder discipline.

Though discipline may hurt in the short-term, it produces an amazing harvest of righteousness in the long-term, encouraging our growth and strengthening our faith. For our discipline to be productive, however, we must exhibit a humble attitude. We do not want to merely endure the discipline or become bitter about it. Rather, we want to willingly accept it and learn what the Lord wants to teach us. Ultimately, the Lord's discipline strengthens our faith and allows us to mature and become the men and women of God we were destined to be.

Day 80
Guarding Our Course

For he guards the course of the just and protects the way of his faithful ones.

—*Proverbs 2:8 (NIV)*

One of the most encouraging aspects of our walk of faith is that the Lord protects and guards the course of the righteous. We see a beautiful example of this in 1 Samuel

25. After spending time in the wilderness, David and his men sought provisions from Nabal, a wealthy man in the area. David and his men had served Nabal by herding his flocks and protecting them from thieves; thus, David's request for provision seemed fair. One would think that out of gratitude, hospitality, or even custom, Nabal would have offered food to David and his men. Not only did Nabal decline David's offer, but he acted arrogantly and rudely, hurling insults at David and his men. This enraged David, and he planned to seek revenge by killing every male in Nabal's household.

Recognizing the imminent danger, a servant hurried to inform Abigail, Nabal's wife. She quickly gave food and drink to David and his men while apologizing for her husband's behavior. She also reminded David that as king he would not want this rash act to taint his reputation. Realizing the wisdom in Abigail's speech, David relented, saying, "Blessed be the Lord God of Israel, who sent you this day to meet me, and blessed be your discernment, and blessed be you, who have kept me this day from bloodshed and from avenging myself by my own hand" (1 Sam. 25:32–33). David had been on the cusp of committing an impetuous and foolish act, but the Lord had stopped him through Abigail.

How encouraging that the Lord protects and guards our course and often intercedes when we stray down the wrong paths. Sometimes the warning comes in the form of a friend's advice; sometimes in the form of an unexpected event that steers our course down a different path. Let's take refuge in knowing that God is for us. He strengthens, encourages, and helps us. Let's listen to all the Abigails in our life and to the subtle warnings that they provide; and let us make biblical choices in our life, thereby bringing glory to our Lord.

Day 81
Lingering in God's Presence

Cease striving and know that I am God; I will be exalted among the nations, I will be exalted in the earth.

—*Psalm 46:10*

Someone once said, "If the devil cannot make you bad, he will make you busy." There is so much truth to the saying, isn't there? The devil wants to sidetrack us in life by keeping us busy, and yet busyness cripples our walk of faith and does not allow us to experience the fullness of what God has planned for us.

Many of us try to keep our faith in God strong, but our busyness creeps in and takes over. Before we know it, we are moving from one activity to another; and the hours become days, and the days become weeks. But what is it that we are really trying to accomplish in all this busyness? What is our true goal in life? If our goal is to know and love God, then maybe we need to restructure our schedules so that we can spend time with him and truly enjoy him instead of being rushed and hurried as we do our quiet times and serve him. We must make time for that which is truly important. We do not want to mistake busyness for real life. Some of our busy activities are clutter, distracting us from our true purpose. When was the last time we did a quiet time and did not look at the clock? Aren't we tired of being rushed and frazzled? Don't we want to truly enjoy God and linger in his presence?

Imagine our life as a glass jar and that we fill it with little pebbles, which represent the more minor things in life. Then we try to fill the jar with three or four big balls, which represent the major things in life, like God, our quiet times, our investment in people, and our service. Unfortunately, there is no more space in the jar for the big balls because the little pebbles have stolen the space. So let's dump out the jar and start again. This time we first place the big balls in the jar, then the little pebbles. This ensures that those things with eternal value are completed and not overlooked because of the seemingly urgent pebbles. We do not want to allow the minor things in life to crowd out the major things. We cannot allow the seemingly "urgent" to take precedence over the truly important.

Day 82
Controlling Our Anger

But I say to you that everyone who is angry with his brother shall be guilty before the court.

—Matthew 5:22a

Anger is a huge hindrance in our walk of faith, and part of the problem with anger is that we possess a cavalier attitude toward it. We think our anger is a little sin and that God will somehow overlook it. We may also attribute our anger to our personality and thus not fully repent when we become unrighteously angry. But anger is not just a part of our personality. It is a serious sin committed against our Lord.

In Matthew 5:21–22, Jesus underscored the seriousness of anger by equating it to murder. Here, Jesus did not say our unrighteous anger leads to murder; he said it is murder. How often do we become unjustly angry with others? It is scary to consider that we may have committed murder in our hearts. Why would Jesus view anger so seriously? Because murder starts with a spark of anger; it starts in the heart. Murder is merely the fruit; anger is its bad seed. Jesus addressed the source of the problem—the heart—rather than the external action, for this is where we defeat sin. If we merely alter the outward behavior without changing the heart, we will remain captive to sin.

If we find ourselves struggling with unrighteous anger, let's choose to extend grace and mercy to those who hurt and offend us. We sometimes expect perfection from others, but there is only One who is perfect—our Lord. Maybe we also need to start giving people the benefit of the doubt. Sometimes we perceive a wrong committed against us when in fact the person has committed no such act. Why waste countless hours stewing over a perceived wrong? Let's also bathe ourselves in the pool of God's great mercy and ask him to create pure hearts in us. God meets us where we are and provides us with the strength we need to move forward in our walk of faith. In the end, either we will control our anger or our anger will control us. Through God, we have the power to control our anger!

Day 83
Comforted to Comfort Others

Who comforts us in all our affliction so that we will be able to comfort those who are in any affliction with the comfort with which we ourselves are comforted by God.

—2 Corinthians 1:4

Scripture describes God as the God of all comfort (2 Cor. 1:4). He is not the God of some comfort, partial comfort, or limited comfort; no, he is the God of *all* comfort. No matter what we are suffering, no matter the pain, no matter the difficulty, God is there to provide strength, encouragement, and assurance. So whether we have lost our job, been betrayed by a loved one, experienced heartache, developed an illness, or just been overwhelmed with life, God is there to provide all comfort. Though our suffering may be great, God's comfort is greater. We can securely rest in God's everlasting love for us and relax in his great compassion.

Scripture further says that God comforts us in our times of trouble so that we can then comfort others. Sometimes, difficulties and trials enable us to empathize with others in a similar situation and provide comfort to them. For example, because my twin boys were born prematurely at twenty-eight weeks, I have always had a special tenderness toward others who have had premature children, and God has given me the privilege of praying for them, encouraging them, and sharing my heart with them. You see, I understand their pain, their difficulties, and their hardships.

Our experiences serve as a reservoir on which God draws to encourage and strengthen others. I have always found it fascinating that Moses spent forty years growing up in the Egyptian palace and then forty years in the wilderness. Then Moses led the Israelites out of Egypt, only to spend another forty years in the desert. We might have complained or even become a little irritable at the prospect of returning to the desert. But God certainly knew what he was doing. After all, who better to lead the Israelites in the wilderness than Moses, who had just spent the last forty years there and had learned the desert's landscape and pitfalls? God brought things back full circle. Sometimes, we experience a season that we may not choose so that God can later use it in our lives to comfort and encourage others.

Day 84
Guarding against Greed

Then he said to them, "Beware, and be on your guard against every form of greed; for not even when one has an abundance does his life consist of his possessions."

—*Luke 12:15*

It is subtle, it is sneaky, and it can destroy the best of us. In one word, it is *greed*, and we are all susceptible to it. In the parable of the rich fool (Luke 12:13–21), Jesus shared a poignant story about greed. A rich man produced a surplus of crops so great that it overflowed his existing barns and raised a perplexing issue: What should he do with the excess? The man decided to do the reasonable thing. He built bigger barns to house the surplus. Seems quite logical, doesn't it? The problem was that the man never sought the Lord's counsel about what to do with the excess. He was focused on himself, his enjoyment of life, and the fulfillment of his needs, ignoring the eternal things. He forgot that riches do not endure forever (Prov. 27:24). Jesus called this man a fool because he gave no thought to eternity. Would we call him a fool or a good businessman?

As the Lord gives to us, he expects and commands that we share with others. He also warns us that our life does not consist of our possessions. Are we sometimes like this man, consumed by our fulfillment and enjoyment? When we receive a bonus from work, do we spend it how we choose or do we first consult the Lord? Do we freely give if the Lord commands it, even if it causes us to sacrifice?

Greed is not really one of the sins that we discuss today, perhaps because it lies secretly hidden in many of our hearts. If we are honest, most of us struggle with greed and the desire for more possessions. So let us be honest with God and let him change the desires of our heart. Let us ask him to help us focus on the eternal and not the earthly. In light of eternity, this life is very short, and material possessions are insignificant unless used for the glory of God. The martyred missionary Jim Elliot said, "He is no fool, to give what he cannot keep, to gain what he cannot lose." Let's make sure we are sending our treasure on to heaven and not trying to keep it in our hands.

Day 85
Enjoying the Preparation Phase

So they said, "An Egyptian delivered us from the hand of the shepherds, and what is more, he even drew the water for us and watered the flock."

—*Exodus 2:19*

Moses was a man of tremendous faith who loved God and humbly served him. He had the privilege of experiencing God in some amazing ways, like parting the Red Sea, receiving the Ten Commandments, and glimpsing God's glory. Moses also had his preparation phase, the season in his life where God prepared and matured him to handle his future service. Sometimes, we want to bypass the preparation phase and skip straight to the action, but the preparation phase is vital because it grows us to handle our future work.

Scripture tells us that Moses spent forty years growing up in the palace but then fled to the Midian desert after he killed an Egyptian. The desert would serve as Moses's preparation place, and he would spend forty long years there; that is approximately 14,600 days—in the desert. It was during this time that God was forging Moses's character. Moses's humility and servanthood grew by leaps and bounds. In fact, Exodus 2:16–19 tells us that Moses even watered some women's flocks. Do you think Moses had ever watered flocks while he lived in the Egyptian palace, enjoying food delicacies and having his whims met? He probably did not; and I think the desert ingrained servanthood on him, preparing him to lead the Israelites. Though some of his preparation may have occurred in the palace, God worked in him in unique ways in the wilderness for forty years. Exodus 2:19 also states that Moses "delivered/rescued" these young women. Here again, another part of his preparation phase. Moses served as a "mini-deliverer" to seven women only to later serve as Israel's great deliverer.[1] God often has us serve in smaller places before he moves us to larger places so we never want to become discouraged when we serve in the small places (or at least, the places we think are small).

I must also stress that rather than just enduring the preparation phase, we want to enjoy it and God's presence. We can certainly try and rush through it, but that usually leaves us frustrated and anxious. Or we can rest in God and allow him to guide us through the preparation phase, enjoying that special time with him and knowing that it will mature us.

Day 86
Choosing to Humble Ourselves before God

I tell you, this man went to his house justified rather than the other; for everyone who exalts himself will be humbled, but he who humbles himself will be exalted.

—*Luke 18:14*

Luke 18:9–14 tells the tale of two men who approached God, a Pharisee and a tax collector. The Pharisee started his prayers focused on himself, using "I" and "me." He thanked God that he was not like other men and proceeded to list all the perceived "good" things he did. Not once did he petition the Lord through prayer; not once did he ask God to help him overcome a weakness. The Pharisee was consumed with himself. Pride is always consumed by self, while humility is focused on God.

Deep in the recesses of our heart lie the tiniest seeds of pride for our perceived goodness. Though we may never verbalize it, some of us think that we are more spiritual than those we know. We may pride ourselves because we do not commit certain acts and then further bolster our opinions of ourselves by listing all the perceived good deeds we perform, like reading the Bible, going to church, and praying. We forget that pride focuses on the faults of others, while forgetting our own faults. We see others' weaknesses but our strengths. Rarely do we compare ourselves to those who excel in our same character trait; rather, we compare to those who struggle in it so we can bolster our self-esteem and ego. If we compared ourselves to the Lord, however, all perceived goodness would be stripped away and we would be stilled into silence. Humility has no place for our perceived goodness. "No one is good except God alone" (Luke 18:19b). Until we realize that nothing good dwells within our flesh and that all good comes from the Lord, we will never exhibit a humble spirit before the Lord.

In contrast to the prideful Pharisee was the humble tax collector. His whole posture and body language denoted his humility. He stood at a distance and did not raise his eyes to heaven. He beat his breast and cried out for the Lord to have mercy on him. Do we understand our spiritual poverty before the Lord? Do we understand that we do not just need a "little" mercy, but great mercy and forgiveness? Jesus ended this parable by reminding his listeners that those who exalt themselves will be humbled and those who humble themselves will be exalted.

Day 87
Fighting the Good Fight

*I have fought the good fight, I have finished the course,
I have kept the faith.*

—*2 Timothy 4:7*

Second Timothy 4:7–8 is considered to be Paul's deathbed statement. Paul wrote Second Timothy as his last letter, and he wrote it in prison during his second Roman imprisonment. Knowing the end was near, Paul reflected on his thirty-some years of ministry. Earlier in his life, Paul had stated his goal to the elders at Ephesus: "But I do not consider my life of any account as dear to myself, so that I may finish my course and the ministry which I received from the Lord Jesus, to testify solemnly of the gospel of the grace of God" (Acts 20:24). Now Paul reflected on his goal, using athletic contests as his imagery. Like a boxer, he had fought the good fight. Like a runner, he had finished his race victoriously. He had kept the faith entrusted to him. Paul had stayed the course, followed the rules, and given his all.

As Paul summarized his life, he described his fight as "good." That is an interesting way to describe his journey, isn't it? The Greek word for good, *kalos*, means "beautiful," "excellent," or "honorable." Why would Paul describe his fight as "beautiful" or "honorable"? Because his fight was for a worthy or honorable cause. This life is full of "fights"—the fight for material possessions, the fight for power, the fight for position, the fight for reputation, the fight to keep friends, and so forth. But none of these are worthy causes from an eternal perspective; none have enduring value. Paul's fight was worthy and noble. It was honorable and would forever bear dividends in eternity. We too must fight the good fight. It is not always easy or comfortable, but it is always worth it because God is worth it. Let us not get sidetracked by insignificant fights. Let us not take up causes that truly do not matter for eternity. Let us fight the *good* fight.

Day 88
Watching Our Words

Let no unwholesome word proceed from your mouth, but only such a word as is good for edification according to the need of the moment, so that it will give grace to those who hear.

—Ephesians 4:29

As a child, I remember hearing the saying "Sticks and stones may break your bones, but words will never hurt you." As an adult, however, I realized the saying is not true. Words do hurt, even more than we can imagine. In fact, words possess great power, the power to help and the power to hinder, the power to encourage and the power to discourage. We must be wise in how we use our words.

Ephesians 4:29 establishes the standard for our speech: we are to allow no unwholesome talk to come out of our mouths. Here is a common speech acronym that has helped me over the years: THINK.

- T – Truthful. Is it truthful? Do we know for sure that our speech is the truth?

- H – Helpful. Is it helpful? Is it edifying to everyone involved in the situation? Will our speech build up the person or tear him down?

- I – Inspiring. Is it inspiring? Does it spur others on to righteousness and holiness?

- N – Necessary. Is it necessary?

- K – Kind. Is our speech kind to the person? Is it spoken in love, with the best of intentions?

If we measured our speech against this standard, we would probably find that we speak far too often. Not everything we think needs to be verbalized. We need to exercise discernment in what we say and talk less. Silence is not always a bad thing. In fact, if we embraced silence more often, our speech would be far more edifying and encouraging. Sometimes we feel awkward during silences and rush to fill them, only to find that we have said something we should not have said. There is a time to speak and a time to remain silent.

To better guard our mouths, we need to pray for our speech and submit to the Holy Spirit. Though we cannot always control our tongue, the Holy Spirit can. The tongue is a powerful instrument, and we must exercise caution in how we use it. We can use our tongue for good or for evil. We can use it to crush and destroy or to refresh and encourage. The choice is ours.

Day 89
Acting Courageously

For we cannot stop speaking about what we have seen and heard.

—Acts 4:20

Sometimes we mistakenly believe that courage means that we are never afraid. But courage is not the absence of fear; it is being bold despite our fear. For example, we may be fearful to share the gospel with a coworker, but courage allows us to speak anyway. Oswald Sanders insightfully noted, "The highest degree of courage is seen in the person who is most fearful but refuses to capitulate to it."[1] Our Christian walk repeatedly challenges us to act courageously, and we want to rise to that challenge. We want to do whatever God commands and go wherever he sends. Whenever we choose to act courageously in our faith, we bring glory to God and impact the world around us.

In Acts 4, Peter and John were forced to appear before the Sanhedrin, the Jewish ruling council, because they miraculously healed a crippled beggar. When asked for further details, Peter responded by saying that they healed the beggar in the name of Jesus and then continued to boldly proclaim the gospel, never watering down its message. The Sanhedrin tried to intimidate Peter and John into silence, but they refused to stop proclaiming Jesus's death and resurrection, saying, "For we cannot stop speaking about what we have seen and heard" (Acts 4:20). Though Peter and John had earlier witnessed their Lord beaten and crucified and knew the same fate could await them, they chose not to succumb to the Sanhedrin's pressure but to act courageously.

We too must stand firm for the Lord and act courageously. Acting courageously means not caving to the societal pressures that surround us. It means upholding the Lord's truth when relativism has become a way of life. It means standing with other Christians and not hiding in the shadows, hoping the difficulty will quickly pass. Many of us may never face a religious trial such as Peter and John, but we have other opportunities to act courageously for our Lord in our homes, at work, with our neighbors, with family members, and with friends. If we want to see God move in amazing ways, we will have to act courageously in our faith.

Day 90
More Than We Can Imagine

Now to him who is able to do far more abundantly beyond all that we ask or think, according to the power that works within us, to him be the glory in the church and in Christ Jesus to all generations forever and ever. Amen.

—*Ephesians 3:20–21*

I love Paul's description of God's power in Ephesians 3:20–21, don't you? God is able to do *abundantly more* than all we ask or imagine. Though it does not translate well in English, in the Greek, the *exceedingly, abundantly more* is a rare double compound to stress its power; in essence, meaning "superabundantly, beyond measure, infinitely more than."

God is not just able to do *all* that we ask

But to do *abundantly more* than all that we ask.

And not just that, but to do *exceedingly* abundantly more than all that we ask!

Most of us have pretty vivid imaginations, but God is able to do even greater works in us than anything we can imagine. In fact, Jesus himself said that believers would perform even greater works than him (John 14:12). Can you imagine doing even greater works than Jesus? And yet, Peter on Pentecost preached the gospel, and over three thousand people believed. Wow! When was the last time we witnessed the power of God like that?

God has untold power to offer us. He transforms ordinary people into great disciples, he gives courage to the weak, and he gives strength to the weary. Whether it is a task that he places before us or a virtue that he needs to grow in us, God will empower us. If we try to live our lives only in our power or depending on our resources, we will fail miserably and, worse yet, become discouraged and disheartened. God has unlimited power to provide us with what we need to meet our daily needs and to accomplish God's will in our lives. It is unimaginable what God can do in our lives if we trust him and walk by faith.

Notes

Day 1: Our Journey of Faith

1. W. E. Vine, Merrill F. Unger, and William White, Jr., "Faith," *Vine's Complete Expository Dictionary of Old and New Testament Words* (Nashville, Tennessee: Thomas Nelson, 1996), 222.

Day 5: Overcoming Unbelief

1. Charles Haddon Spurgeon, "The Sin of Unbelief," *Spurgeon's Sermons*, Delivered January 14, 1855, www.spurgeon.org/sermons/0003.html; accessed May 5, 2015.

Day 6: Leaving a Legacy

1. Frederick C. Mish, ed., "Legacy," *Merriam-Webster's Collegiate Dictionary, eleventh ed.,* (Springfield, Massachusetts: Merriam-Webster, Incorporated, 2003), 710.

Day 7: Embracing God's Truth

1. A. W. Tozer, *An Anthology,* ed. Harry Verploegh (Camp Hill, Pennsylvania: Christian Publications, 1984), 181.

Day 16: Victorious in the Warzone

1. Spiros Zodhiates, ThD, gen. ed., *The Complete Word Study Dictionary New Testament* (Chattanooga, Tennessee: AMG, 1992), #3823, 1091.

Day 27: God's Silence Is Not His Absence

1. Oswald Chambers, *My Utmost for His Highest Updated Edition* (Grand Rapids, Michigan: Discovery House, 1992), October 11.

Day 32: Embracing True Greatness

1. A. W. Tozer, *Born After Midnight* (Camp Hill, Pennsylvania: Christian Publications, 1989), 50.

Day 38: Living without Reservation

1. Dave Jackson, Neta Jackson. *Christian Heroes* (Wheaton, Illinois: Tyndale, 2005), 270.

Day 48: Living without Scheming

1. Warren W. Wiersbe, *Be Authentic* (Colorado Springs, Colorado: ChariotVictor Publishing, 1997), 14.

Day 50: Prevailing in Prayer

1. Zodhiates, *The Complete Word Study Dictionary New Testament*, #335, 150.

Day 56: Refusing to Settle for Mediocrity

1. Charles R. Swindoll, *Living Above the Level of Mediocrity* (Nashville, Tennessee: W Publishing Group, 1989), 11.

Day 57: Our True Inheritance

1. A. W. Tozer, *The Pursuit of God* (Camp Hill, Pennsylvania: Christian Publications, 1982), 19.

Day 60: Remembering God's Past Faithfulness

1. Brett Dutton, "Introduction to Judges," Classroom lecture notes, OLDTS 3313S—Basic Old Testament I, Southwestern Baptist Theological Seminary, Fall 2014.

Day 61: The Snare of Man

1. Warren Baker, DRE and Eugene Carpenter, PhD, *The Complete Word Study Dictionary Old Testament* (Chattanooga, Tennessee: AMG Publishers, 2003), #7682, 1100.
2. Ibid., #4170, 585.

Day 63: Strengthened by the Holy Spirit

1. A. T. Robertson, "Romans 8:26," *Robertson's Word Pictures in the New Testament*, http://www.studylight.org/ commentaries/rwp/view.cgi?bk=44&ch=8 (May 5, 2015).

Day 64: Ensnared by Envy

1. Vine, "Envy," *Vine's Complete Expository Dictionary of Old and New Testament Words*, 1996), 204.

Day 73: Persevering in Our Faith

1. Zodhiates, *The Complete Word Study Dictionary New Testament*, #5281, 1425.

Day 85: Enjoying the Preparation Phase

1. Charles R. Swindoll, *Moses* (Nashville, Tennessee: Word Publishing, 1999), 64.

Day 89: Acting Courageously

1. J. Oswald Sanders, *Spiritual Leadership* (Chicago, Illinois: Moody Press, 1967), 55 as quoted in R. J. Morgan's *Nelson's Complete Book of Stories, Illustrations, and Quotes* (electronic ed.), (Nashville, Tennessee: Thomas Nelson Publishers, 2000).

Bibliography

Baker, Warren and Eugene Carpenter. *The Complete Word Study Dictionary Old Testament*. Chattanooga, Tennessee: AMG Publishers, 2003.

Chambers, Oswald. *My Utmost for His Highest.* Updated ed. Grand Rapids, Michigan: Discovery House, 1992.

Dutton, Brett. "Introduction to Judges." Classroom lecture notes, OLDTS 3313S—Basic Old Testament I. Southwestern Baptist Theological Seminary. Fall 2014.

Jackson, Dave and Neta Jackson. *Christian Heroes.* Wheaton, Illinois: Tyndale, 2005.

Mish, Frederick C., ed. *Merriam-Webster's Collegiate Dictionary*. Eleventh ed. Springfield, Massachusetts: Merriam-Webster, Incorporated, 2003.

Morgan, R. J. *Nelson's Complete Book of Stories, Illustrations, and Quotes.* Electronic ed. Nashville, Tennessee: Thomas Nelson Publishers, 2000.

Robertson, A. T. "Robertson's Word Pictures in the New Testament." StudyLight. Accessed May 5, 2015. www.studylight.org/commentaries/rwp/view.cgi?bk=44&ch=8.

Spurgeon, Charles Haddon. "The Sin of Unbelief." *Spurgeon's Sermons.* Delivered January 14, 1855. Accessed May 5, 2015. www.spurgeon.org/sermons/0003.html.

Swindoll, Charles R. *Living above the Level of Mediocrity*. Nashville, Tennessee: W Publishing Group, 1989.

Swindoll, Charles R. *Moses*. Nashville, Tennessee: Word Publishing, 1999.

Tozer, A. W. *An Anthology*. Edited by Harry Verploegh. Camp Hill, Pennsylvania: Christian Publications, 1984.

Tozer, A. W. *Born After Midnight*. Camp Hill, Pennsylvania: Christian Publications, 1989.

Tozer, A. W. *The Pursuit of God*. Camp Hill, Pennsylvania: Christian Publications, 1982.

Vine, W. E., Merrill F. Unger, and William White, Jr. "Faith," *Vine's Complete Expository Dictionary of Old and New Testament Words*. Nashville, Tennessee: Thomas Nelson, 1996.

Wiersbe, Warren W. *Be Authentic*. Colorado Springs, Colorado: ChariotVictor Publishing, 1997.

Zodhiates, Spiros. *The Complete Word Study Dictionary New Testament*. Chattanooga, Tennessee: AMG Publishers, 1992.

Made in the USA
Middletown, DE
15 April 2016